I0234336

The Traditional Side by Side

"Part Two"

King of the Upland Bird Guns

By Doug Stewart

Copyright © 2020 by Doug Stewart

All rights reserved. No part of this book may be reproduced in any manner without the express written consent of Doug Stewart, except in the case of brief excerpts in critical review or articles.

This book was published by Doug Stewart and proudly printed in the United States of America.

Loveland, CO
970-443-1124
dougstewartauthor@gmail.com

Website: dougstewartauthor.com
Facebook: Doug Stewart Author
Instagram: @doug_stewart_author

10% of all profits will be donated to:
Hunters for The Hungry (hfth.nra.org)

Table of Contents

The Traditional Side by Side

King of the Upland Bird Guns

"Part Two"

<u>Forward</u>

I never planned on part two. I have had so many requests for a part two that I can't believe it! My Website and Facebook page are visited constantly. I hear all the feedback and questions. The subject of side by sides and upland bird hunting is a never-ending open book. I really appreciate each and every person that has supported my book! Come join the side by side Renaissance in part two.

The Traditional Side by Side

King of the Upland Bird Guns

"Part Two"

Preface

In my first book I regret not thanking my Lord and Savior, God. Nothing would be possible without my faith in Him. I am thankful for my wife, family, friends, and my audience (new friends). The side by side enthusiasts that I have met have been amazing people. There almost seems to be a special code of honor among the gentlemen that love double guns. I'm thankful for the whole upland bird hunting family. May God bless you all and may the family continue to grow.

Make as many memories as you can... your memories are all you will have when the Autumn of your life arrives!

Section I

"Another Memorable Hunting Trip"

Many years ago, my friend Tony and I took our fathers bird hunting in Choteau, Montana. After researching my Blacks Wing and Clay book, this seemed like the best bet for Hungarian Partridge and sharptail grouse. Mind you this was back in the mid 1990's and I did not have a computer, so it took a lot of phone calls and a Blacks book. This was going to be my first bird hunt in Montana, and I felt so fortunate to take it with my special father!

I will always cherish the memories I made with my father in Choteau.

We left super early on a Friday morning and both our dads seemed very excited to go. Tony had recently purchased a big dooly Ford truck and wanted to drive. The drive was going to be a long one, approximately 12-15 hours I believe. Back in the mid 1990's Montana's main interstates had no speed limit during daylight hours. Tony had the pedal to the floor and thank God the truck had a governor that would kick in and not allow the truck to go over 99 miles an hour. Tony was mad, but I think the rest of us were glad. We pulled into town at approximately 7:00 pm and called the outfitter, Hank, right away. Hank was surprised we made it so quickly, we were not. We decided to eat at a little pub across the street from our hotel. I remember talking my dad into drinking a beer with me. My dad doesn't drink, so this was a special trip to relax and unwind.

Here is the whole crew on our trip in Montana.

After dinner and several beers later, we went to the hotel. The hotel was very cool with stuffed animal heads on the walls and the old rustic log look. The place even had an indoor pool that my dad kept looking at. After unpacking, my dad had a crazy idea. He said, "let's all go swimming then sit in the hot tub." This was not the crazy part. None of us had swimsuits. My dad said, "who cares, let's all go in our underwear." My dad figured no one was around, and we were in the middle of nowhere (maybe the beer was talking). In the pool we went, acting like kids, splashing each other, jumping in, etc. It was so neat to see our dads acting like kids having fun. What a great start to a memorable hunting trip. Hank met us early Saturday morning at the hotel. We followed him for miles heading west out of town. Eventually we drove back on a little dirt road to three cabins on a small lake. The views were to die for, mountains to our left, hay fields to the right, and a gorgeous lake at our doorstep. I had finally made it to big sky country to hunt.

Hank showed us the main cabin with the big kitchen. He told us that the kitchen was fully stocked with food and to help ourselves when we wanted as it was self-serve (just the way I like it). Next, he took us to our cabins. I had arranged for a guide just for the first day. Hank told us that Dennis would be there shortly to guide us and show us where we could hunt the other days. Now came the rules from Hank, "I have a few rules for you men: eat anything you want, fish, shoot anything you want that's in season, you'll see that you'll be able to hunt almost anywhere, be safe, and above all have fun."

We all settled in at our cabin and got our hunting gear ready. Tony's dad, Dibbi, pulled out his two shotguns for him and Tony to use on the hunt. Both guns were 16 gauge doubles. One was a very well engraved Merkel and the other was a Sauer. Both guns were very light weight and pre-world war quality. Dibbi was my kind of guy. I brought my new CSMC Fox CE 20 gauge and my old faithful L.C. Smith 3-E 16 gauge. My father brought the only gun he ever shoots now, a nice Ruger Red Label 28 gauge that I gave him. The guide, Dennis, pulled up to the cabins and got us all together and started talking about our hunting strategy. He seemed to be a quiet man that didn't say much.

These are my two special side by sides that I made all my memories with in Montana.

We started hunting in a valley at the base of the mountains, the field had an interesting variety of native grasses and looked prime for sharptails. The field was heading us toward a little river that was flowing down the entire side of the mountain as far as the eye could see. When we got to the river my dad and I took one side, and Tony and Dibbi took the other with Dennis. My dad was walking next to Russian Olive trees at the river's edge.

I stayed about twenty yards from him on the edge of a wheat field with plum thickets between us. I was anticipating a covey of Huns to explode at any moment, instead my dad kept flushing doves out of the trees right over me. I couldn't take it anymore, so I mounted my 20 gauge and shot a dove. Almost instantly a covey of about six sharptail grouse got up. I panicked and took a shot. Clean miss, my dad started ribbing me, "wow, we drove almost eight hundred miles to shoot a dove." After cleaning my pants out, I said, "Those sharpies only flew about a hundred yards up the river, let's go after them and I'm going to get a good head shot on one for redemption." My dad laughed and told me to dream on. After about ten minutes of walking, my dad busted the covey. We both only shot once as they jumped a little wild. Two grouse fell. My dad picked his up, I hollered over to him to pick mine up. He didn't see mine drop but I did. After a few minutes he found my bird and held it up in the air and said, "You smart aleck, it's shot right in the head." We continued up the river with great shooting as we seemed to be pushing birds back and forth with the guys on the other side of the river.

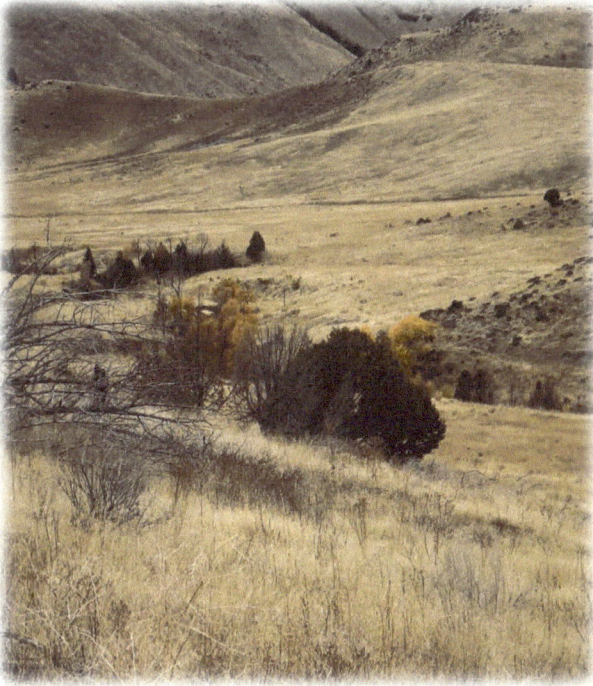

This is the perfect Hun and sharptail country!

Finally, Dennis stopped us and called for us to come over to him. Dennis pointed to some large bear tracks in the mud. He said they were fresh and that his dog could get mixed up with the grizzly and bring the bear back to us. The dads were getting hot and tired anyway, so we decided to go back to the cabins for lunch. After lunch Tony and I decided that we wanted to try and shoot some snipe as we had bumped a few coming back to the cabins. My dad and Dibbi said they would like to take a nap. The guide was done for a half day hunt, so Tony and I were on our own. The west side of the lake was a big swamp and part of the field by it was filled with a few inches of water. An absolute snipe heaven! As you may or may not know, Snipe do not fly in a straight line like most birds, they zig and zag all over the place. The shooting was a crazy blast, I used all of my 20 gauge ammo. All I brought was 7 1/2 shot, so some of the snipe were in rough shape. After the fun we went back to the cabin and found our dads out on the lake in a boat fishing. My dad caught one of the biggest trout I have ever seen. The dads were having a blast on that little lake. Both were laughing and acting like best friends. When the evening rolled around, I pulled out my L.C. Smith and we all got some good dove shooting in as doves came into the bank of the lake on the east side for a drink. It was about the third week in September and in one day we shot Huns, sharpies, snipe, and dove, and caught some fish. What a day in big sky country! I'll never forget my dad and me sitting in lawn chairs watching the sun set in the sky, he said two distinct things to me, one was "it doesn't get any better than this," and the other thing he said was, "how can anyone see this beauty and not believe in God." I made a point to drink a cold beer every night while I sat by the lake watching the sun set. I woke up each morning with a hot cup of coffee and sat in the same place right out of the cabin by the lake to watch a spectacular sunrise. This was the most peaceful way I have ever started and finished every day in my life. We were surrounded by beauty in every direction. Three days went by without seeing another person. The air was so clean and fresh, at night the stars were so bright, with nature's sounds of frogs and crickets. No sirens, no dogs barking, no traffic, just peace. I was stress free, I could think clearly, it was a pure religious experience. This is what upland bird hunting with your father is supposed to be all about! A rich tradition that I am grateful to still have in our country. Why would I want to take a memorable hunting trip like this with anything but a traditional side by side?!

The Montana sky was truly beautiful.

Side by sides have always been and will

always be... king of the upland bird guns!

Section II

A. "The Side by Sides Superiority in The Uplands"

I'll start right off by saying that I'm only claiming that a side by side is superior to other shotguns when the gun is being carried and quickly mounted to shoot in any condition at various angles. I do not claim that a side by side is superior when pre-mounted. Most people will shoot an over and under better at clay pigeons when the gun is already mounted. A side by side is designed to be shot in a swinging mount and fire technique. Side by sides are faster and have a lower moment of inertia. This allows a shooter to mount the gun faster, to change directions quicker and easier, and to be able to focus on the bird. A side by side is balanced to naturally work with your reflexes. All shotguns have a single sighting plane but a side by side seems wider to our peripheral vision. The shallow receiver puts the hands close to the same plane as our eyes which can really help us to quickly adapt to any flight pattern of the bird. A narrow sighting plane of the over-under is most precise against a clear background such as when shooting clays. The broad sighting plane of a side by side is much easier to see with a background of brush such as when hunting woodcock and grouse.

The Traditional Side by Side

"Part Two"

You should never aim a shotgun, but your eyes will see a sighting plain for a fraction of a second in your peripheral vision. An over-under can be easier to point precisely when pre-mounted and feels more like a rifle. The consensus is that an over-under is better when pre-mounted and a side by side is better when the gun is not pre-mounted, and I agree. One last thing that I have noticed on this subject, I believe that a side by side is more difficult in manufacturing to perfectly regulate barrels and point of impact than an over-under. This is the reason I only shoot best-grade doubles. Best-grade side by sides are expensive and most people form their opinion only after shooting a cheap, poorly manufactured side by side. You need precision when shooting targets like clays. An over-under is easier to regulate and to build in general. The bottom line is that over-unders are much cheaper to build and to purchase, and are available everywhere in many different brands. As most things in life, money is the determining factor. A quick little fact to ponder on, the world famous All-American trap shooter, Herb Parsons, used a side by side. What about Annie-Oakley or Lord Ripon? I guess they all used a quality made side by side. Remember, an over-under was made before side by sides. The side by side was preferred by the top game shooters in the golden age of shot gunning. Just a little food for thought.

A perfect example of a superior side by side.

Always hunt with a gun that is sentimental

to you... the uplands are sacred!

Section II

B. "The Other Great Shotguns of The Uplands"

The cat is out of the bag, I have the side by side disease. But I must say, there have been several different kinds of shotguns that have been iconic and very important in the uplands. Side by sides are very special, but I think it's important to use the gun that you can shoot well and enjoy the privilege of upland bird hunting with. This subject reminds me of a hunting story I must tell, and the story also makes a great point or two that we can all learn from.

Many years ago, I met a gentleman in the gym that loved to hunt. I found out that he had grown up in Nebraska and was a bird hunter all his life. Naturally, every time I saw him in the gym, we would end up talking about bird hunting. One year when October was approaching, he asked me if I wanted to go pheasant and quail hunting with him in Bartley, Nebraska. I was so excited that I could hardly even spit out the word, "sure!" Both of us were in our early twenties and full of energy. This was going to be a trip to remember forever!

We got a cheap hotel in McCook, Nebraska and split the cost as we were going to hunt for a few days. Bartley was really close to McCook, so the drive was easy to make each day. My friend had family in Bartley and had permission to hunt thousands of acres. The first morning of hunting we pulled up to an old barnyard to park the truck and unload our guns. He pulled his gun out for the hunt...I was totally speechless! The gun was a Winchester model 1897 pump 12 gauge. He handed the gun to me and said, "Feel this baby, I have shot this gun my whole life and it is worn in like an old comfortable pair of slippers." I was thinking, "worn in", more like "worn out and going to fall apart." This gun was uglier than a homemade bar of soap. Let my description paint a picture of this gun in your mind. The 28-inch barrel had the bead sight missing, and the

"Part Two"

barrel was silver with rust pitting and I even noticed a couple of little dents. The pistol grip had duct tape wrapped around the smallest part and the wood was badly marred. The gun did mount well and reminded me of the feel of my grandfather's old Model 12. With the exposed hammer and all the cosmetic damage, it just looked old and worn out. He took the gun back and told me that the stock cracked when he was shooting teal earlier in the year and that the tape would hold it until he had time to glue and pin it. He also proceeded to tell me that it was extra full choke and that he could hit anything with it. I just didn't know what to say, I think all I said was "great." Then I reluctantly pulled out my gun, which was an AYA model number 2 sidelock 20 gauge. For the first time on a hunting trip I felt bad, kind of like a spoiled brat. Thank God he didn't treat me this way, as I handed him my gun. He said, "Wow, this gun is light, kind of weird looking, but kinda cool." I could tell that he could care less about my gun, and that he loved his old pump. This made me feel comfortable and not so bad. I was very confident in my shooting ability with this gun. I'll talk more about this little AYA later in this book.

We started walking down a dirt road next to the bar ditch. My friend told me that there was a covey of quail that liked this old ditch and to pay attention. The field that we were going to hunt was about one-half mile or so down the road. The road started to curve, and we were going to enter the edge of a corn field right at the curve. Several large cottonwoods lined the bar ditch right at the curve. Almost as soon as I stepped in the bar ditch to cross it a covey of quail exploded. I was caught off guard and only got one shot off. One quail dropped in good condition because I only hit it with a couple of No. 6 pellets. Now for my friend, his model 97 sounded like a chain saw. Two quail were blown to smithereens, and a third dropped way out in the corn field. Wow, a triple on quail with a pump. I had never seen such a thing! Two of the quail were so well centered that they almost were disintegrated, and the third was stone dead out in the field about 40-45 yards away. This was not a fluke, the same kind of shooting saga continued for three days. I shot well for me, but my friend schooled me! Here is the total breakdown in three days. I missed one bird that was an easy shot, and my friend shot across the field and nailed it. I also had one pheasant cripple that took off running down a corn row and my friend shot it right in the head at 30 plus yards while it was running full speed. On the last day we came across a big ravine at the end of a corn field. The ravine was full of brush and plum thickets. My friend stayed on top of the ravine and blocked while I walked into it. Pheasants exploded out of it, with hens and roosters going every direction. I pulled a double, and my friend ran his chain saw and dropped three roosters. My friend never missed a shot in three days, and every bird was stone dead when he shot, with some looking like they were hit with a grenade launcher. All I can say is amazing, it was like he was Annie Oakley or something. I had pure respect for him, and the conversation driving home was totally different than the conversation driving out there! I asked him how he learned to shoot like that and what some of his concepts were on shooting technique. I kept my mouth shut and listened to the best shot I had ever seen in my life. He said that there were two key factors to his shooting. One was being able to focus to an extreme level. He went on to say that his focus on the bird is so intense that he loses all the background and all surroundings, and can only see the bird in great detail, and that everything seems to be in slow motion. The second key factor was to be able to point quickly and precisely. He said that all this happened gradually from an early age. I asked him to explain this evolution. I could tell that he was excited that I cared and wanted to hear all about it. He told me that his first gun was a BB gun, and he would go down by a bridge and shoot water skippers and dragonflies out of the ditch. Being bored in Nebraska meant shooting all day long. Eventually he got so good that he could shoot dragonflies as they were flying.

The Traditional Side by Side

"Part Two"

The ability to just point and shoot became natural, and so did the obsession with shooting anything flying. At about the age of 11 his father got him a single shot 22. By the age of 12 he could just point and hit a duck flying up out of that old ditch. The next progression was his father giving him his personal Winchester model 1897 12 gauge for his birthday. This was the only shotgun he has ever shot. Now for practice he said that he shoots barn swallows and starlings. He said that this old gun put the food on the table when growing up, and that he even shot two deer with it using 00 buck. I could tell that shooting only one gun and knowing exactly where it would shoot was very important to him. I truly believe his stories, and two things he said became engraved in my mind and in my own technique of instinctive shooting. I now practice and believe in working on my focus and pointing ability more than anything. I love double guns, but I want to apologize if I ever offended anyone with a different kind of gun. I am thankful for all the great guns and their manufacturers. Someday maybe I'll add to my collection with a Browning Superlight 20 gauge, or a sweet sixteen, maybe a Winchester Model 12, 16 gauge. The list could go on and on. Just get out and enjoy the great privilege of upland bird hunting!

Section III: Three Special Gauges Revisited

In my first book I discussed six different gauges and the advantages each gauge has in the uplands. I feel that three of these gauges need to be revisited with great respect and honored as their designs are ingenious. Hunting the uplands means walking miles on end, the gun you carry will be held in the ready position for hours upon hours and shot very infrequently. As ounces begin to feel like pounds, a lightweight double is a delight to behold. A fast gun can mean the difference between making a clean shot on a bird or not even getting a shot off. The 16 gauge, 28 gauge, and the 2-inch 12 gauge are very comfortable to carry, very light and fast, and produce low recoil with deadly patterns. Did I mention that they are graceful and elegant looking? I would love to see a comeback of these special gauges as they have added pleasure to my bird hunts in a traditional way. These little gauges define a true bird gun.

True gentlemen shoot 16 gauges in the uplands.

Section III: Three Special Gauges Revisited

A. 16 Gauge - The Ultimate Upland Small Bore

In my life I have shot more birds and hunted the most often with a lightweight 16 gauge. Never have I felt under-gunned, or over-gunned when using light loads. In my first book I talked about the square load with one ounce of shot, and the great patterns they produced. Now I often use 7/8 oz. loads anytime I'm shooting a 7 1/2 shot size or smaller. Last season I shot my Parker CHE 16 gauge with 7/8 oz. of 8 shot at doves and these loads proved to be absolute dynamite. I had minimal recoil, super short shot strings, a clean bore, and very efficient kills as far as I am capable of shooting. Make sure you use a lightweight 16 gauge between 5 1/2 – 6 lbs. The beauty is that your gun can be lighter than most 20 gauges, pattern better, with less recoil. Stick with 2 1/2-inch loads with 1 oz. of shot, or 7/8 oz. of shot. These loads will have low-pressure and recoil and will burn clean with great game-getting patterns! When walking the prairies in Montana, a lightweight 16 gauge is so perfect. The gun feels just right in your hands and is comfortable to carry for miles on end. When birds flush, the 16 gauge will be fast and capable of long shots if needed. In my last book I talked about O Frame Parker 16 gauges and Fox 16 gauges. I want to mention that you can find a gem in a lightweight English 16 gauge, or a Francotte, or even a pre-war Sauer. If you're into pumps, the Winchester model 12 pump 16 gauge is great. I would love to see the comeback of the ultimate small bore!

A lightweight 16 gauge that is properly scaled to size is always the right choice in the uplands! The 16 gauge is the queen of the uplands and will never be dethroned!

This is my Bently and Playfair 16 gauge built on a 20 gauge frame.
Weighing only 5 lbs 10 oz.

When a gentleman reaches his full maturity

in the uplands... he shoots a 28 gauge!

Section III: Three Special Gauges Revisited

B. 28 Gauge - The Little Gauge That Performs

In my last book I talked about the perfect relation between the 28 gauges bore: .550 and a ¾ oz. of shot. The square load is ideal just like the 1 oz. loads in a 16 gauge bore. Both produce great patterns with short shot strings. We all know this now, but I feel there is something more. Dangerous game hunters know about the magic of the 375 H&H Magnum. They know that there are rifle cartridges out there that produce more velocity than the 375 and produce more energy with a heavier bullet. But other rifle cartridges can penetrate too much or too fast, and not do enough damage. Other loads make a big hole but do not penetrate deep enough to the vitals. A 375 H&H Magnum has a balanced ability to penetrate to the vitals, make a big wound channel, and leave all its energy in the animal. The balance cannot be quite figured out by performance data, but hunters know its magic with clean kills. I give this example because I feel the same magic with a 28 gauge. I know it has great patterns and short shot strings, but I used ¾ oz. loads in my 20 gauge and the 28 gauge performed better. I believe a 28 gauge is more efficient with cleaner kills than a 20 gauge out to 30 yards. This is a big claim, but I have shot both gauges for nearly 40 years killing thousands of birds. Several years ago, I decided to go on a 28 gauge only odyssey. This odyssey lasted for two years. I made a commitment to only shoot 28 gauges, one was a Parker Repro and the other was a Merkel 280 EL (which I wish I still owned). In these two years I shot woodcock, ruffed grouse, doves, pigeons, Bob White quail, gambles quail, scaled quail, pheasants, sage grouse, Hungarian partridge, sharptail grouse, blue grouse, snipe, and chukars! So, let's say that I have experience with 28 gauges. Small bores do not pattern large shot sizes well, so make sure you pattern your gun. The largest shot size that I achieved great patterns with was number 6 shot. Both guns loved Federal Premium Magnums with ¾ oz. of copper plated number 6 shot. This was my pheasant and sage grouse load. I do not recommend a 28 gauge for all around pheasant hunting, but I was killing them stone dead out to 35 yards! A strange thing, when I was cleaning the pheasants, the No. 6 shot had better penetration than any 6-shot I had ever shot a pheasant with, and I mean with my 12 gauges. I also had better percentages of kills on doves, woodcock and grouse. Maybe it was due to low recoil, or the easy handling gun. In any case, I can say that I was never under-gunned and had clean kills. The 28 gauge like the 375 H&H Magnum I compared it to, both perform better than they should, and I don't think there is only one explanation. The 28 gauge has many great attributes: it's light weight; the slim feel in your hands; fast handling with low recoil; small, light shells in your pockets; the pure elegance in appearance; and the deadly patterns. To enjoy all the special attributes, find a 28 gauge that weighs between 5 1/2 to 5 3/4 pounds, and shoot 3/4 oz. loads of small shot. My friend and mentor Michael McIntosh would roll over in his grave if he knew that they were making a 3-inch load of dynamite for the 28 gauge now! Do not try to make the little gauge shoot further with big loads. This ruins all the magic. Give a 28 gauge a try with my guidelines and you will see that the 28 is the little gauge that performs.

As I have grown older, I can see why the 28 gauge is considered the gentlemen's gun of choice. The gentlemen in the north woods know this, and the gentlemen in the southern piney woods know this. The 28 gauge is a treasure that I hope more people discover!

My AYA model #1 28 gauge. A Spanish best sidelock built in 1997 in the pinnacle of Spanish best made guns. The little beauty weighs 5 lbs 4 oz and has all the bells and whistles. Handmade highly polished locks with gold plated internals, fine scroll engraving, rolled edge trigger guard, hinged front trigger, hand detachable sidelocks, disk set strikers, double locking underlugs, gas escape valves, gold line cocking indicators, highly figured French walnut, Wow!

This is my James MacNaughton 28 gauge.

Refined gentlemen shoot 2-inch 12 gauges.

Section III: Three Special Gauges Revisited

C. 2-Inch 12 Gauge - The Legend that Needs to be Resurrected

The 2-inch 12 gauge is the third gauge I'd love to see used more in the uplands. The wonderful little gauge never was big in the U.S. for a couple of reasons. First and foremost, no U.S. gun maker manufactured a 2-inch 12 gauge, which I understand as the cost to make one would be cost prohibited. Americans have a different value and concept of money and quality than the English. After my 28 gauge odyssey, I went on a one year 2-inch 12 gauge odyssey. Starting with dove season, I shot every bird all season long with only my 2-inch 12 gauge. My 2-inch 12 gauge only weighs 5 lbs. and is balanced better than any gun I have ever owned that is this light. The little gun has a Churchill rib, great trigger pulls, skeet chokes, and feels great in my hands. The short shot string was deadly on crossing shots at doves, and the quick handling gun was useful. The next season for me were Huns and sharptails.

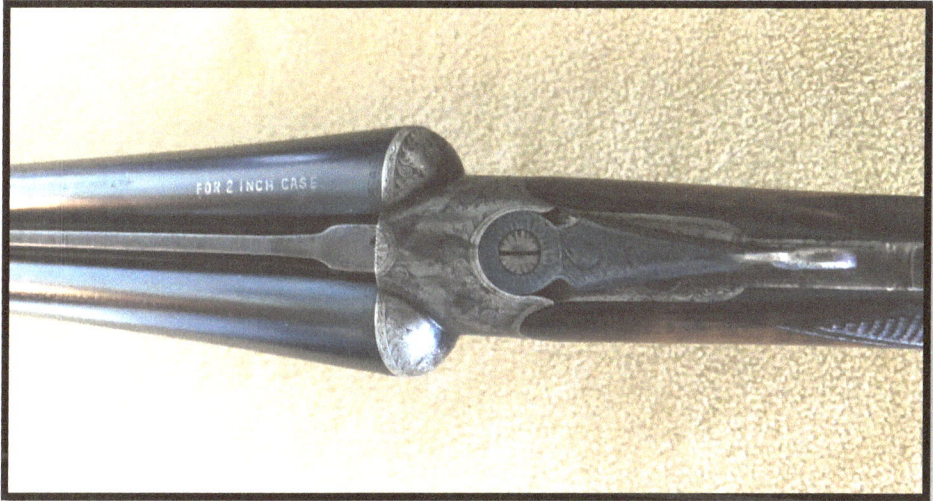

This is my 2-inch 12 gauge.

"Part Two"

I used a 15/16 oz. load of 7 shot from RST. Zero cripples, the birds fell out of the sky like they were struck by lightning. Next came woodcock hunting. I used a 7/8 oz. load of 10 shot from RST. It seemed like I was throwing a handful of sand at them, or a big fly swatter just swatting them out of the air. Honestly, I do not remember missing a single woodcock and they were all dead before they hit the ground. I switched to a 7/8 oz. load of 8 shot for grouse. All the birds died in the air with a cloud of feathers floating down from the sky. Next came the true test, pheasants. This is the toughest bird in the uplands, so I used a 15/16 oz. load of 5 shot in the left barrel and 15/16 oz. load of 6 shot in my right barrel. Both loads were from RST. I kept my shots to 35 yards max and the birds dropped with authority. The penetration on the birds was amazing, and the shocking power of short shot strings seemed to stop the speedsters from running. The rest of the season I shot a few different species of quail, all with 7 1/2 or 8 shot, and all with a great kill ratio. After patterning my 2-inch 12 gauge extensively I knew my one-year odyssey would go well, and I must say the little gun just kept impressing me more and more. Now I can give a very complete and accurate review of the 2-inch 12 gauge. I believe the great penetration was due to the fact of less deformed pellets. The small payload of the 2-inch load in the large .729 bore of a 12 gauge means less bore scrub on the pellets which can deform the pellets and cause them to fly poorly and lose all their energy very quickly. Also, the low pressures that the 2-inch load produces does not have as much set back pressure upon firing like other loads, and set back pressure damages a lot of pellets. The result is that you end up with a very beautiful pattern of nice round pellets flying with great energy to penetrate. Now we take in account that all the pellets arrive at the target at the same time in great shape, this is the ultimate shocking power. When I would hit birds, you could literally see the bird being pushed through the air. Another great attribute is that the 2-inch 12 gauge is not fussy about shot sizes like small gauges. Most 28 gauges will not pattern well with larger shot sizes, usually they start to pattern poorly with anything larger than 7 1/2 shot. My 2-inch 12 gauge produces great patterns with everything from 10 shot to 5 shot. My English 2-inch handles so nicely in the uplands and is lightning fast. This could be the ultimate upland gun.

This is my good friend Robert Zielke's 2-inch 12 gauge. He routinely shoots woodcock and grouse with this gun and believe me, he is a refined gentleman.

Many years ago, Jack Jansma from Wing Shooting Adventures had Arrieta make him a run of a hundred 2-inch 12 gauges. I had to buy one. The gun was beautiful, it was a sidelock with 27" barrels and you could order your own stock dimensions and you had a choice of chokes. I loved the look and idea of the entire project. However, I feel that this was just not a true 2-inch 12 gauge in a few aspects. My gun weighed 6 lbs. The barrels were thick and proofed for much heavier loads. I did not like the balance or the weight of the gun. The whole idea of a 2-inch 12 gauge is to get a very fast, light gun that patterns great. I own a 5 lb. 14 oz. 16 gauge that is very fast and well balanced, so why should I have a 6 lb. 2-inch? I sold my Arrieta and got an English 2-inch 12 gauge and have been happy ever since. Now I ride the struggle bus between using my 28 gauge or my 2-inch 12 gauge. The only logical thing to do is to take them both for a walk in the woods so one of them doesn't get jealous. The 2-inch 12 gauge needs to be resurrected in the uplands!

Section IV: Patterning Your Shotgun

My grandfather was the first person to teach me about patterning a shotgun. He was very adamant about it and would say, "You have to know where and how your damn gun is shooting!" When I grew older and matured, it was then that I realized how important it was to pattern your shotgun. Would you go predator hunting without sighting your rifle in? No, or you could miss every shot. A shotgun could be even more important to shoot at a target than a rifle, and at least tell you more factors of performance. Many different things can be learned from shooting a target with your shotgun. The first thing that is most commonly mentioned is how tight the pattern is. The second is usually how well the gun shoots to the point of aim. Less mentioned but important is how high or low the pattern is. The pattern should be examined for a lovely even spread without large empty untouched areas in the middle of the pattern. Birds can be well centered in your pattern and fly through these holes untouched or worse, they could get crippled. Look for flyers way out on the edges of the target, these are cripplers that usually are a result from long shot stings (the shot is deformed). Once you get your gun to perform as you desire, you must pattern the loads that are going to be used on your hunt. Shotguns all have pet loads. Use the loads that pattern the best, always!

About 30 years ago I owned an AYA model #2 20 gauge. The right barrel was choked skeet, and the left barrel was choked tight improved cylinder. I shot load after load trying to find a perfect pheasant load. The little 20 gauge had terrible patterns with any No. 4 shot or No. 5 shot. The patterns had holes in them everywhere, and too many fliers on the edges. Finally, I found a No. 6 shot load that was amazing. This little gun loved Federal Premium copper-plated No. 6 shot in 1 oz. loads. I could not take a piece of paper and draw a better pattern on it by hand than this gun would print with this load.

"Part Two"

A hummingbird could not fly through this pattern, and the coverage was even and spread in a perfect concentric circle. The results on the patterning board were self-proving in the field. I shot more pheasants in the four-year period that I owned this gun and with this load than the rest of my life. The pheasants were stone dead when I hit them. With a shotgun, the pattern is what kills the bird. The shocking power of multiple hits, with due regard of penetration is the magic bullet in shot-gunning. Without patterning your gun on a patterning board, everything is just a guess.

Now I must give one more story about the importance of patterning your shotgun that I just encountered about a month ago. I know a gentleman that lives in Kansas that has become a very good friend of mine. We both love side by sides, dogs, and bird hunting. My friend was buying a Holland and Holland 16 gauge, and was consulting with me about the gun. When he received the gun, my friend took all the measurements of the barrels in great detail, (chambers, bores, chokes, and wall thickness). My friend and I both had a few reservations about the barrels. I told him to go pattern the gun and call me. First off, he shot at some clay pigeons, then he shot the gun at a 30-inch circle at 40 yards. I got a phone call from him saying it was the strangest thing ever. He went on to say that he could hit the targets with his left barrel but was missing them with his right barrel. The good old patterning board told the story. The left barrel was shooting to the point of aim with 60% of the pattern above the center and 40% of the pattern below. This is a perfect game-getting pattern that he is used to shooting. Now for the right barrel. The entire pattern was off to the right and below the center. Wow, the Holland and Holland had been altered from the original factory configuration by a less than competent gunsmith! I think this makes my point on the importance of patterning your gun. My friend is selling this beautiful gun that is as worthless as a glass hammer.

There are several ways to pattern a shotgun. I'm going to share with you the ways that have worked for me and what can be learned from my techniques with patterning your shotgun the different ways that I pattern them. First off, make a simple frame onto which a large sheet of paper can be stapled to for the purpose of determining choke performance. Make the paper target height about the same height as your shoulders. The industry standard is to shoot at the target at a measured 40 yards, then draw a 30-inch circle around the largest concentration of pellets, count them, and determine the percentage of pellets from the entire load that are within the circle. I have all the different pattern percentages in detailed graphs in my first book. An example is that a 70% pattern at 40 yards equates to a full choke. Now you know how to determine the actual choke your gun has. The next type of patterning to shoot will determine if the gun shoots to the point of aim, and how high or low the gun will shoot. I take a large piece of paper and draw a 30-inch circle on it. Now I draw a smaller 15-inch circle inside of the 30-inch circle. I'll color in the 15-inch circle so I can see it well at 40 yards. Back up 40 yards and really steady your gun. Aim your shotgun (the only time I will ever tell you to aim a shotgun) at the center of the 15-inch circle and fire. Several pellets should strike the center depending on your choke, but the entire pattern should be straight in line with the 30-inch circle. Most upland bird hunters like to have 60% of the pattern above the dead center and 40% of the pattern below the dead center. This is a great balanced pattern for birds that are slowly rising off the ground. When shooting game such as chukars that fly downhill, a 50/50 pattern may be preferred. Some driven game bird shooters like a 70/30 pattern, this is all a personal preference. A skilled gunsmith can slightly alter your point of impact that the gun shoots by the way he opens your choke, but you need to have plenty of choke to work with and a skilled gunsmith! Patterning is also useful in gun fitting. Once you master a perfect gun mount and have a gun that seems to fit well, the patterning can begin. Take your normal 30-inch circle target and back up exactly 16 yards from the target. Concentrate on the marked aiming point (center), shoulder the shotgun and quickly fire. After many shots a general trend should emerge from the patterns. Measuring from the very center of the aiming point, each inch of displacement of the pattern translates to a stock adjustment of 1/16 inch. This is the real way to fit a shotgun. With this method of gun fit, the shotgun will shoot where one looks, with your own personal style of gun mount. One last style of patterning I'll do is to shoot at phone books to test for penetration. On some game birds like pheasants this is important. With smaller, thin-skinned upland birds, this is not an issue. Usually I will not shoot at a pheasant much beyond 35-40 yards, so I shoot at the phone books at 35 yards. I remember when testing that AYA model number 2, 20 gauge that I talked about earlier, I found two brands of ammunition loaded with 6 shot that had great even patterns. One was the Federal Premium copper plated 1 oz. load of 6 shot, and the other was a Remington Express 1 oz. load of 6 shot. The Federal was my ultimate choice because of the phone book test. The Federal load was more consistent in general, and the Federal load had a lot better penetration every time I shot at the phone book. The results on the patterning board and phone book helped me to find the ultimate pheasant load for my little 20 gauge!

I can't stress enough the importance of patterning your shotgun. Your success will go up in the field and you will cripple fewer birds. You will learn your gun and be able to make the proper adjustments. I know patterning is very time consuming, but the art and science of shot-gunning can be very useful and fascinating. Follow my advice in its entirety from this book and you will be very successful in the uplands with your classic side by side!

Section V: Chokes and Cartridges

After the last chapter on patterning your shotgun it is fitting to talk about chokes. In my last book I had graphs with the different constrictions designated for all the different gauges. I'm going to give a few more of my observations and opinions about chokes after 40 years of shot-gunning.

First, you need to understand what choke means and what it does for your pattern. The choke section in a shotgun barrel is at the muzzle and it shapes the shot charge. The constriction usually starts to take place anywhere from 1 to 2 1/2 inches from the muzzle. Gunmakers measure the constriction in thousandths of an inch. Americans define various chokes as cylinder, skeet, improved cylinder, skeet II, modified, improved modified, full, and extra full. The British define various chokes as cylinder, quarter, half, three-quarter, and full. There are several different types of choke, the ways in which they are cut into the barrel vary in design.

A tapered (conical) choke simply has a gradual taper all the way to the muzzle. This type of choke is a simple, easy choke to create, and the most common.

A conical parallel choke has a tapered section first, followed by a parallel section, usually about an inch in length maintaining the desired constriction. The conical parallel choke is usually found on high-class shotguns and is harder to design and regulate. Some of the best patterns can come from this design of choke.

Jug (recessed) chokes are cut into the bore just behind the muzzle. This type of choke is used to restore some choke to a shortened shotgun barrel. This is very rare now that screw-in chokes can easily be installed.

Bell (special skeet choke) choke is rare, but the old skeet shooters know all about it. The desired constriction takes place about 2-inches from the muzzle, then about ¾ of an inch from the muzzle the bore is reamed out larger than the largest diameter measured throughout the bore. For example, if you have a 20 gauge that has a bore measurement of .615, it may measure .625 at the muzzle. The effect is similar to shooting a spreader load out of a skeet choke.

Then there are the good old screw-in chokes of today. As you can probably tell, I despise screw-in chokes. In all fairness, I will explain why along with the good, bad, and ugly of the screw-in choke madness. There is no arguing that screw-in chokes are fast and convenient. A shotgun can be versatile when any choke can be used out of one gun. New choke tubes can handle any hard, non-toxic shot with ease, and the extended tubes can add length to your barrel if you need it. Screw-in chokes add weight to the end of the barrels, which some people may claim helps their swing.

I get irritated when hunting with someone that is constantly changing their chokes out. This kills the argument of how fast and convenient choke tubes are. My side by sides have two different chokes at all times, and I can select either one with an instant choice of a trigger pull! One shotgun should not be used for every type of bird one can hunt. A goose gun should be heavy to handle heavy loads. A quail gun should be light as to be fast with and to carry all day. Trying to say that one gun can do everything just because it has screw-in chokes is in a word, "rubbish." The fact that choke tubes must have such a hard steel to handle non-toxic shot that is harder than most gun barrels is crazy. When pellets are this hard, they have bad characteristics. Pellets that are overly hard will easily ricochet, over-penetrate, and have poor energy transfer into the game. Overly hard pellets will pattern too tight at close range and will often have a blown pattern. Open chokes with hard lead shot have the best patterns for close range upland gunning. The thick and hard inconsistent choke tubes are not necessary. My friend and I measured several choke tubes. It was unreal to me that the tubes were not consistent in measurement or even concentric. An improved cylinder could measure anywhere from a skeet to a modified and still be stamped as an improved cylinder. You never know the exact measurement in thousands of an inch that you will be getting with a choke tube when you order one. Screw-in chokes that are totally machine made in mass quantities will never match the precision that a skilled craftsman can accomplish by hand with a reamer and emery cloth! Ask yourself why a best-quality English side by side will not come with factory installed screw-in chokes, end of story. Keep in mind that adding weight to the muzzles is awkward and the wrong way to distribute weight to a lively bird gun.

I think it is a shame when I see a gentleman pull out a very expensive gun on a hunt and it has two ugly screw-in chokes sticking an inch and a half out of the muzzles. I can't get over how out of place and ugly they look, the entire gun takes on a cheap, modern look to it. I hope that my view on screw-in chokes will resonate with a few people, and I'm sure it will stir up controversy, my specialty!

Now that we have some education on what chokes are and what they can do for our pattern, it's time to decide what is the best constriction for upland gunning in our fine double guns. Upland bird hunting should be a close-range affair. Shotguns are deadly close-range weapons and are not intended for long range. Do not take irresponsible long shots. Often a bird will fly off and look as if it was totally missed only to die later from a single pellet wound. I personally keep my max range to 40 yards and cripples are few and far between for me. With all this said, I believe that very little choke is needed in the uplands. Being over-choked is a serious handicap, remember that most birds are missed by a small margin. How much choke if any is really needed out to 30-35 yards? My motto is to put the largest pattern out there with regards to distance and use the smallest shot size possible with due regard of energy needed for a clean kill. My favorite set up in my side by sides is skeet I and skeet II chokes. Take your own trap thrower out to shoot some clays. Use a skeet choked gun and throw some slow close-range targets. After you smash them consistently, start shooting them farther and farther away. It will shock you how far you can crush a target with a skeet choke. The old wives' tale that a full choke will either miss or kill is wrong. I have seen many a bird hit in the tail with a full choke and fly off crippled. A skeet choke would have covered the bird from head to tail with pellets. The tight choke syndrome that you see on clay target courses is unnecessary and can result in misses on game birds. Clay target shooters are competitive and have egos, they get ribbed if they do not smoke the target, and they hit so many targets that it starts to come down to who hit the target harder. You do not want to smoke a prized game bird that you worked hard for. This year my wife and I took a late January pheasant hunt in eastern Colorado. I knew that the shots were going to be the longest of the season and I still took a shotgun choked skeet and improved cylinder. All I did to get a little tighter pattern for the long shots was to use different ammo than I normally use. I used a load of B&P MB nickel plated No. 5 shot. I shot three roosters with three shells. All the birds were dead before they hit the ground at 35-40 yards. When you open your chokes, you will see your success rate go up in the uplands. In my last book I had recommendations for choke selection and shot size selection for almost every type of upland bird in North America. Please reference my first book for this data and for the data on the different designated constrictions for each choke.

Now that you know how to get the desired pattern out of your shotgun and where your gun is shooting, it makes sense to use great cartridges. Cartridges were covered in my last book, so I will cover a few different topics that I did not cover previously. The first is the dreaded non-toxic shot. Bismuth is the closest alternative to lead. Bismuth has almost the same characteristics as lead in weight and hardness. Bismuth is slightly lighter than lead and can be prone to shatter if loaded to high velocities. My testing has been limited due to the extreme cost of RST Bismuth cartridges. I realize that the new RIO Bismuth cartridges are more affordable, but RST is the only low-pressure Bismuth loads I can find for old side by sides at $65.00 a box. The loads that I have shot pattern tightly and perform like lead out to almost 40 yards. Beyond 40 yards, lead is king. Now for steel shot, I do not recommend its' use out of fine old doubles. Steel shot is just too hard for old barrels and the new loads produce too much pressure for lightweight bird guns! Steel is effective if you go up two or three shot sizes from your normal lead size, but the load will contain fewer pellets. Remember that the smaller steel shot pellets will cripple birds at long range. The steel high velocity, high pressure loads commercially available are only usable in heavy modern shotguns. All the other loads that are effective, like heavy shot, and the various tungsten loadings are all high pressure loads of dynamite and expensive. So, what is the answer for a great non-toxic load? My answer is not to put the cart before the horse. Americans did just that many years ago. Let me explain. I remember many years ago when lead was banned for all waterfowl hunting. Steel was the only option at the time, and steel shot loads were not perfected yet. The number of crippled birds from steel was like the plague. We tried to be conservationists by stopping lead poisoning and killed three times as many birds by making a law without a better solution proven to work before the law was instituted. Do not let the lobbyists band lead shot in the uplands without a great low-pressure alternative to lead, that can be used in all guns. Wildlife will take a huge hit in the uplands if lead shot is banned right now. Lead will not kill upland birds, the lack of money from hunters will. If I and all the side by side enthusiasts put our doubles away and quit hunting the uplands, it would be catastrophic. Think about it, I buy a hunting license for every state I hunt in. I am a member of almost every upland bird conservation organization that exists. Besides donating our money, we donate our time. My wife was part of a woodcock banding program in Minnesota last year, and I helped on a quail habitat project. Banning lead shot in the uplands will not save upland birds, saving habitat will! We need all the sportsmen's money to go toward habitat conservation. It's the animal activists and antigun lobbyists that are not using their money for habitat. Remember what happened to our woodcock population because of activists against logging. Do not let the tail wag the dog. Gulf courses, private lakes, subdivisions, and the general encroachment of urban living is what wipes out wildlife, not lead shot! Let's focus and spend our money and time preserving wildlife habitat. Currently, several major shotgun shell manufacturers will go out of business with a total lead band. If I can logically think all this through, what makes you think that antigun activists haven't thought all this through? Next thing you know the activists will want to band steel shot because it's too hard and breaking animals' teeth, causing them to starve to death (ha, ha). Let's be patient and find a way to produce Bismuth at an affordable cost, for all guns!

Now moving on to the great lead upland loads. The English understand high quality cartridges and shoot birds as a way of life. Americans are caught up in high pressure magnum cartridges. I wish we could learn from the English. Quantity is not quality and a high velocity load will not be more effective on game. In Great Britain there have been more pheasants, partridge and grouse shot with low-pressure 2 1/2-inch cartridges than anywhere in the last century. I believe in the art and science of ballistics and realize that shotguns shoot round projectiles that have different characteristics than a bullet. In the bullet world speed kills, in the shotgun world excessive speed ruins a great pattern. Remember that a pattern is what kills the bird, not a couple of fast pellets. It is a fact that the faster you start a round projectile, the faster it will slow down due to atmospheric resistance. And the more it slows down, the more energy it sheds. I have achieved some of the best patterns with loads leaving the muzzle at 1200 fps. Then when I crank up the muzzle velocity to 1330 fps the pattern goes from great to horrible. Extra velocity really only adds enough extra energy at a game-getting distance of 35 yards to kill a dragonfly. A load of No. 7 1/2 shot leaving the muzzle at 1330 fps will only be moving about 30 fps faster at 35 yards than a load of No. 7 1/2 shot leaving the muzzle at 1200 fps. The only one who gets hit noticeably harder is the guy shooting the gun. Now that we have dispelled the myth of the effectiveness of high velocity loads, there is one more argument in favor of high velocity loads I hear often. This argument is that high velocity loads require less forward allowance. Is this argument true? Yes, all of two inches less, which is not really something to get excited about when you're dealing with a pattern about three feet across. The real reason that high velocity or magnum loads seem to work well for some is simply the fact that the individual has confidence in the load. When a person has confidence, it is natural to use our subconscious, which is an instantaneous response, which results in perfect calculated shooting. When you do not have confidence, your conscience takes over trying to calculate, and the time delay can result in a miss. I have had several sessions with professional shooting instructors and all of them used low-pressure loads that produced mild velocities and low recoil. Recoil is the real demon to consistent shooting! I was crushing the targets and in turn, I have confidence in low velocity loads. There are two overwhelming reasons why high velocity loads are popular or even exist. Uneducated individuals will refuse to believe that less can be more. The American belief is bigger and more powerful is better. I fell for the false advertising when I was young. A box of shells that say high velocity load with extra knock-down power, extended range, etc., looks and sounds like the best. The second reason for the loads that kick like an old mule is to aid in the proper functioning of auto loaders. Pattern your shotguns as I discussed in the previous chapter and you will become a believer. The best way to deliver extra down range energy on game birds is to increase the size of the pellet, not the velocity.

For a handy reference, I designed a pellet count chart for various shot sizes in an ounce of shot. Then I listed a velocity chart for standard commercially available loads. Next, I designed a chart to help choose a proper shot size and choke for different game birds. Lastly, I listed some great options for low-pressure loads designed for lightweight guns and superior performance. I hope the different guides will be helpful!

Chokes and Cartridges

Normal Pellet Count Per Ounce of Lead Shot

Shot Sizes	1 ¼ oz	1 1/8 oz	1 oz	7/8 oz	3/4 oz	1/2 oz
No. 4	169	152	135	118	102	67
No. 5	213	192	170	149	128	85
No. 6	281	253	225	197	169	112
No. 7	437	393	350	306	262	175
No. 8	513	462	410	359	308	205
No. 9	731	658	585	512	439	292

American and British Shot Sizes

American Designation	Diameter	British Designation	Diameter
4	.13"	4	.12"
5	.12"	5	.11"
6	.11"	6	.10"
7	.10"	7	.095"
7 1/2	.095"	7 1/2	.09"
8	.09"	8	.085"
9	.08"	9	.08"

Handy Conversion Charts

American Shell Lengths	English & European Lengths
Imperial or Standard	Metric
2 3/4"	70mm
2 5/8"	67mm
2 1/2"	65mm
2"	60mm

American Shot Charges	English & European Shot Charges
1 1/4 oz	34 grams
1 1/8 oz	32 grams
1 1/16 oz	30 grams
1 oz	28 grams
7/8 oz	24 grams
3/4 oz	20 grams

NOTE: European shells appear to have higher muzzle velocities. But, remember that they test the muzzle velocity right at the muzzle. Americans acquire muzzle velocities at three feet from the muzzle. This could make as much as a 100 FPS difference. Velocities of Common Factory Loads.

Gauge	Dram Equivalent	Shot Charge	Muzzle Velocity FPS
12	3 1/4	1 1/4	1220
12	3 1/4	1 1/8	1255
12	3	1 1/8	1200
12	2 3/4	1	1180
16	3	1 1/8	1240
16	2 3/4	1	1220
16	2 1/2	1	1165
20	2 3/4	1	1220
20	2 1/2	1	1170
20	2 1/2	7/8	1200
28	2 1/4	3/4	1295
28	2	3/4	1200

"Part Two"

Chart for Upland Bird Hunting

Game Birds	Proper Gauge	Shot Charge	Lead Shot Size	Suggested Chokes
Pheasants	12,16,20	1 oz & up	4,5,6	SK,IC,M,IM
Grouse: various species	12,16,20	1 oz & up	6,7,7½	SK,IC,M,IM
Partridge (Ruffed grouse)	12,16,20,28	3/4 oz - 1 oz	7½,8,9	Cyl,SK,IC
Quail: various species	12,16,20,28	3/4 oz - 1⅛	7,7½,8	SK,IC,M
Bob White quail, Mearns quail	12,16,20,28	3/4 oz - 1 oz	7½,8	Cyl,SK,IC
Woodcock	12,16,20,28	3/4 oz - 1 oz	8,9,10	Cyl,SK
Snipe	12,16,20,28	3/4 oz - 7/8 oz	9,10	Cyl, SK
Dove	12,16,20,28	3/4 oz - 1⅛ oz	7½,8	SK,IC,M
Pigeons	12,16,20,28	3/4 oz - 1⅛ oz	7,7½	IC,M
Hungarian Partridge (Huns)	12,16,20,28	3/4 oz - 1⅛ oz	7,7½	SK,IC,M
Chuckar	12,16,20,28	3/4 oz - 1⅛ oz	6,7,7½	IC,M

NOTE: Always use high quality ammo with extra hard shot that patterns well in your gun when hunting game birds! This is the way of true gentlemen. Birds deserve no less! Improved modified is the tightest choke needed with today's ammo, a full choke can give you a blown pattern.

Shot Load in ounces	IMP Mod Choke 65% +	Mod Choke 60%	IC Choke 50%	SK Choke 45%	Cylinder 40%
1¼ oz	45 yards max	43 yards max	40 yards max	37 yards max	34 yards max
1⅛ oz	42 yards max	40 yards max	38 yards max	35 yards max	30 yards max
1 oz	40 yards max	38 yards max	35 yards max	32 yards max	28 yards max
7/8 oz	38 yards max	36 yards max	33 yards max	30 yards max	26 yards max
3/4 oz	36 yards max	34 yards max	30 yards max	27 yards max	24 yards max

This chart is designed to help aid in choosing the right load for your bird hunt. The maximum consistent killing range is designated for each choke to achieve clean kills. The distances were determined using only high-quality ammo that uses plastic shot cups containing extra hard lead shot. Keep in mind that (on average) 90% of all upland birds are shot between 15-35 yards and should be!

"Part Two"

Manufacturers of High Quality, Low-Pressure Ammo

Made for Fine Old Doubles and Gentlemen

1.) <u>RST</u> #570-553-1651 <u>or</u> RSTShells.com
Comments: Morris Baker owns RST and is a good man, a true side by side enthusiast. Morris and I had a great talk about Parkers and 2-inch 12 gauges over the phone just a couple months ago. Morris has been very supportive of my book and the entire side by side world. Thank you, Morris! RST is the gold standard in low-pressure ammo with the widest selection of shells for every gauge and shot size imaginable. I use RST all the time!

2.) <u>PolyWad.com</u> #800-998-0669 Vintage Ammo
Comments: Don't be fooled by the small selection. PolyWad produces top of the line low-pressure ammo. Just great low recoiling ammo with great patterns.

3.) <u>William Larkin Moore & Sons LLC</u> #480-951-8913
Comments: Always 7000 PSI max or lower for every load. These loads kill birds! Thunderbird loads the ammo and uses some of the hardest shot available. The shells are clean burning, have low recoil, and are devastating on birds. I love them!

4.) <u>Holland & Holland</u> #360-736-0089
classicshooting.com
Comments: I shoot some of their true 2 1/2" paper 1 1/16 oz. 12 gauge loads that have fiber wads. This particular load is great for close range work as it produces large even patterns.

5.) <u>Gamebore</u> (Kent) Various retailers carry them. I have purchased them from Woodcockhill.com #570-864-3242
Comments: Gamebore loads generally have fiber wads and produce larger patterns. The loads burn clean and use hard diamond shot that penetrates well. Gamebore

loads have higher velocities than the other manufacturers I have listed, and more recoil! Use the shells with the smaller shot charges, as they produce lower pressures.

*If you can find an importer that carries English loads (2 1/2), they are great loads! Eley, Hull, Lyalvale Express

The Traditional Side by Side

"Part Two"

I feel that traditional side by sides should be shot using gentlemen's low-pressure loads. I have personally taken it even further and I now shoot paper loads with fiber wads 70% of the time. RST has great paper loads with or without fiber wads. For the nostalgic side in us, these loads can stir happy associations in our minds. The fact that our forefathers shot side by sides with paper loads and enjoyed the smell of smoke from freshly burned gun powder can be enjoyed by us just the same. We all have certain happy associations from the things we see, hear, and smell. This can be as simple as smelling freshly brewed coffee in the morning or the smell of a campfire. After I fire a paper load and break my double open the smoke rolls out of the chambers and fills the crisp fall air in the woods with the sweetest smell of gun powder ever. This proves that some things never change and that the good times can still be now. I have heard claims from some experts that paper loads produce lower chamber pressures, less felt recoil, and are biodegradable (except for the brass head). Honestly, it's all about the smell and the cool sound fiber wads make for me. One word of caution about shooting paper loads, they can be as addictive as having to have a cup of coffee in the morning.

It is natural to enjoy the things we are good at!

Section VI: Another Look at Shooting a Side by Side Properly

Properly shooting a side by side was discussed in my first book with great passion. When my book came out, I was featured on a few podcasts. People started emailing me, following me on Facebook, calling me, etc. With all the feedback, I had more interest and questions about instinctive shooting than any other subject. My goal is to delve into the subject and renovate a few basics, and to prioritize the most important aspects of shooting a side by side. With instinctive shooting many experts will put a priority on different aspects of the technique. I am going to discuss a couple of forgotten factors that I believe are very important for long term consistency in game shooting.

Here I am shooting my side by side properly at quail.

These are the rewards of using the proper technique!

Section VI: Another Look at Shooting a Side by Side Properly

A. Factors to Shooting a Side by Side Consistently on Game Birds

In this section, I am going to discuss five different factors that I believe are the keys to becoming a great game shot with a side by side. Any person will benefit from this passa ge with any gun, but a side by side is king of the upland bird guns! Some people will benefit more from a certain factor of shooting techniques and others will not. I used to think gun fit was one of the most important factors in shooting great, and now that I am older and can shoot almost any gun (within reason) I have put more of a priority on being able to focus and point well. Everyone is different so read this section carefully and master the ways of shooting a side by side like a true traditional upland bird hunter!

Section VI: Another Look at Shooting a Side by Side Properly

A. Factors to Shooting a Side by Side Consistently on Game Birds

    1. The Right Technique Using "Perfect Practice"
       A. The Foot Position

Every structure needs a foundation. A shooter not solidly balanced on his feet is not going to be very successful at hitting game birds. The right foot position is a fundamental part of properly shooting a game gun. Your feet should be in the same plane as your hips, shoulder width apart, with the leading foot slightly in advance and pointing right to where you are going to kill the bird. The leading foot should be bearing the majority of your weight.

Spreading your feet far apart is useful if you're practicing the splits or some other gymnastics. The wide stance feels stable but isn't necessary and is very restrictive. To be able to shoot a moving target, you need to be flexible in your waist and ankles. You cannot do this unless your feet are fairly close together and lined up with your hips. If your stance is wide you will soon reach the limit of your ability to pivot, get bound up, drop a shoulder, and swing the gun in an arc that will pull the muzzle off the line of the bird's flight. You must get squared up to the target and be in balance. By practicing over and over a simple foot technique can become automatic.

Always start with your feet together as the first movement in the swing-and-mount sequence. Next, you step with your leading foot toward the target, a small step, no more than eight inches. When your foot goes to the target, followed by your leading hand, everything comes together at once. By stepping forward you will be physically and mentally ready for the target with your weight on the proper foot and your body will be in balance with the proper positioning to move the gun in any direction.

This simple step method is very easy but effective. Try with some targets first, you will be amazed. Remember to put your feet together first, then step and mount in a swinging smooth movement, and the targets will start to break just from having the right foundation!

Section VI: Another Look at Shooting a Side by Side Properly

A. Factors to Shooting a Side by Side Consistently on Game Birds

      1. The Right Technique Using "Perfect Practice"
         B. The Ready Position

In the last chapter we discussed foot position. Now, the next part to practicing with the right technique is the ready position with good posture. A good golf swing is built from the ground up, and the same is true for swinging a shotgun. Now that our feet and body are properly set, we can move up and build a physical relationship with the gun.

I have had several sessions with different shooting instructors over the years and they all would say lift the gun to your cheek without moving your head, and I agree. Keeping your head still is crucial. Your head must serve as a solid point of reference to point accurately. If you keep your head still, your eyes will have a stable foundation to properly focus and calculate. Watch someone that is missing target after target, you'll most likely see him slamming the gun butt to his shoulder and dropping his head to the stock while chasing the target.

If you have your feet set correctly in the right position with balance as we discussed in the last chapter you won't have to move your head. This is the key, everything works together. Your body is ready to receive the gun.

Now for your posture, stand up straight with your knees barely bent so your quads are solid and flexed. Your weight should be toward your leading foot, with a slight bend forward at the hips. This is a solid body position that isn't over exaggerated but does put the upper body in position to receive the gun without moving anything but your arms. Do not contort your body like you see others doing at the clay range!

"Part Two"

Many top-notch shooters look more awkward than a three-legged cat trying to bury a turd on a frozen pond. This is great for circus freaks, but not for bird shooting. Keep relaxed and comfortable.

Now you are ready to bring the gun to the ready position. Simply tuck the butt of the gun under your right armpit. Your left hand should be on the fore end so that your left arm will be well extended when you mount the gun. Remember to point the barrels with your left hand. Both of your elbows should be angled out and down. Keep the entire gun level to the ground.

This ready position accomplishes many things. First, it eliminates the need for extraneous movement. Second, the barrels are continually in your peripheral vision. This allows you to guide the barrels to where they need to go without taking your eyes off the target. Lastly, it forces you to push forward with your leading hand instead of your right hand. This push forward is a key element to the entire motion you want. Practice at home and at shooting clays so it will happen automatically.

Section VI: Another Look at Shooting a Side by Side Properly

A. Factors to Shooting a Side by Side Consistently on Game Birds

    1. The Right Technique Using "Perfect Practice"
        C. The Gun Mount

      Now you are ready to swing and mount. These two movements always go together in this sequence. Your first move should be with your leading hand, and it should start the barrel moving onto the flight line of the bird. This first move is the beginning of the swing. Let the actual mount follow from that. This needs to be one motion, not two! Mounting the gun first and then tracking the target is a big mistake and requires two moves; swing and mount is only one smooth movement. The only exception to this rule would be a dead straight away shot. This is very rare as almost all shots have a bit of angle involved. Practice the swinging mount in your house, yard, etc. Follow straight lines as moving objects follow a specific line of flight. To recap shooting with the right technique, your feet are about shoulder width apart, the leading foot pointed to the spot where you plan to kill the bird and bearing most of your weight. You're bent slightly forward at the hips; your head is slightly tilted down so the gun can hit the cheek without moving anything but your arms. Your leading hand is extended out on the forearm or further, and the butt is tucked under your armpit. The first move is with your leading hand pushing the gun forward out of your armpit. Your elbows are pointing out and down. Now you smoothly swing and mount the gun painting a line through your target, and fire when you pull in front and keep swinging. Believe me when I tell you this is the right technique and remember that perfect practice makes perfect!

Section VI: Another Look at Shooting a Side by Side Properly

A. Factors to Shooting a Side by Side Consistently on Game Birds

2. The Right Gun Fit

This is the second factor in shooting a side by side with consistency on game birds. Now that we are using the right technique when shooting, you need to have a gun that fits you. I know that we all have guns that do not fit us well, and we can still shoot them decently with some minor adjustments in how we handle them. I'm very guilty of this because I love to collect (accumulate) as many different side by sides as possible. I cannot have every gun altered to fit me. Sometimes I'm over-confident in my shooting abilities and they fail me. When the shooting gets fast and furious in unforgiving terrain you need a gun to shoot exactly where your eyes are looking with no unnecessary extra adjustments. You will shoot more consistently and cripple fewer birds using a gun that fits properly, period, end of discussion!

In my first book, I gave you height charts for L.O.P. and some other general guidelines for gun fit. I must reiterate that we all have a very individual build to our bodies. I still recommend a couple of professional gun fittings. This gives you a base to work from. No one can guess your exact measurements over the phone or by your height and weight. When I help someone, it must be in person. Many shots are fired at targets and a patterning board. The gun needs to be mounted properly and with consistency, that is why I wrote the chapter on the right technique first. After a lifetime of shooting side by sides at upland birds I have my own opinions on gun fit, but it took professional fittings to get me close, and to understand what measurements give a certain cause and effect. Having a gun that fits you like a glove will put more birds in the bag for you, give you less feeling of recoil, and it will work naturally with your reflexes. It is advised to shoot one gun like my friend did in chapter two, advice that I'll give but never take myself as life is too short to only enjoy one gun!

Section VI: Another Look at Shooting a Side by Side Properly

A. Factors to Shooting a Side by Side Consistently on Game Birds

3. The Right Balanced Gun

My first book had a very in-depth chapter on gun balance. I will not repeat the chapter, but I want to add a few more suggestions. I'm a shorter man with a fairly small structure. By nature, I have very fast reactions and am fast in general. I had to learn the hard way that against the recent fad of long barrels and heavier guns, I shoot great with guns that are light and have short barrels. A fast gun works naturally with my genetics. Believe it or not I now shoot a 2 1/2" 12 gauge that has 25" barrels with a Churchill rib that only weighs 5 lbs. 15 oz. With this gun I can shoot almost as good as I did over twenty years ago. This little English sidelock is very light and well balanced, it allows my natural reactions to take over like they should.

This is the Arthur Hill 12 gauge that only weighs 5 lbs. 15 oz. This is a very well balanced English upland game gun.

Now let's examine someone with a different build to their body and has different genetics. My Uncle Mike who hunts with me is six feet tall, lanky, and is very slow in general. Mike is a great shot, but he is slow and smooth moving. By the time he gets on the bird, the bird is flying fast and further away than when I shoot. A slightly heavier gun with longer barrels keeps his gun swinging to work with his body and style of shooting. My little guns feel whippy to him and he stops swinging on the longer shots that he takes. A fast-starting gun stops fast. I move fast and shoot my birds at close range before they pick up speed and become difficult to focus on. This is natural for me but not for Mike. This is what I mean by having the right balanced gun for you and your style of shooting. Don't get me wrong about 25-inch barrels. I think Churchill shotguns have a magic feel and handling qualities that are perfect for me in the uplands, but it's not because of the 25-inch barrels, it's because of the balance and feel Churchills have. We should be looking at the bird not the barrels, so the barrel length does not matter! What does matter is how much the gun weighs, the balance point, and how the gun reacts with your natural reactions. Don't be at odds with your gun. The right balanced gun for you will be comfortable to carry and shoot, it will effortlessly point where you look, and compliment your style of shooting to where it will happen naturally without having to think about it. Would you wear boots on your hunting trip that did not fit well, or shoot rifle slugs out of your shotgun at quail? Well, the right shotgun is just as important to a successful hunt as your boots and ammo!

Section VI: Another Look at Shooting a Side by Side Properly

A. Factors to Shooting a Side by Side Consistently on Game Birds

4. The Right Speed and Rhythm

In my last chapter on the right gun balance I mentioned how I was fast by nature and my Uncle Mike was slow by nature. Now that we are going to use a well-balanced gun that is comfortable and balanced to suit us as an individual, we need to get the right speed and rhythm when shooting game birds.

Many years ago, I was lightning fast with a shotgun. This was all fine and dandy until I started missing with the first shot and nailing the bird with my second shot on a regular basis. This all came to a head one day after a very embarrassing incident. Mike and I took off to go take our ritual pheasant hunt out east. We stopped at a farmer's house that we go to once a year. As always, the farmer gave us permission to hunt. This particular property is only about 100 acres with a gnarly patch of plum thickets and little junipers in one corner of the field. The corn had been cut and plowed under, so we decided to walk across the plowed field and still try to find something at the other end in the plum thicket patch. Mike had his gun over his shoulder, and I had my gun at my waist as usual. I remember talking about a strategy to use on the plum thickets as we walked across the plowed field casually. Suddenly my foot jerked up and a loud cackle with a flurry of feathers fluttered up in a whirlwind right in front of our faces. I was so startled that I freaked out and shot my gun off my hip in self-defense. The pheasant exploded about 10 feet in front of us. Mike and I literally looked like we had been tarred and feathered. I had never seen so many feathers floating in the sky as the breeze blew them all in our face. The pheasant had been almost completely disintegrated and we were both in shock. What in the world just happened? I'll try to explain this terribly unjustified reaction to a poor defenseless bird that I foolishly employed. As I explained in the previous paragraph, I had been shooting too fast on my first shot. My barrels were not swinging properly in the flight path of the bird until my second shot, and this was making me jumpy. Now with my new-found jumpiness, I freaked out and reacted by shooting a pheasant that was threatening my life. This was a very embarrassing incident that Mike has not let me live down, and now everyone knows about it. I told this story for three reasons: one is that I deserve the teasing I receive; two, is that I'm making a point; and three, is that the story is true. I just got used to reacting as fast as I could, and when I stepped on the pheasant's tail, I lost my mind.

Now we understand what I mean when I say that we need to develop a certain speed and rhythm when shooting a shotgun, often called being steady to flush. I personally think being fast in the uplands is important. I usually bag more birds than my hunting partners because I'm alert, ready, and fast. I get cleaner kills with the closer range I shoot at, and the birds haven't picked up as much speed allowing me to focus on the head more precisely. This is all great if I have the right technique and my barrels are swinging through as I shoot. I had to slow down and be steady to the flush until I had just the right speed and rhythm to shoot where the bird was going to be, not where the bird was. Developing this timing is easier than it sounds, but crucial to consistent shooting. So, I needed to slow down, but too often I see shotgunners going too slow and taking too long to shoot. Being too slow can pose a few problems. The first problem I see often is that when you move too slow you end up slowing your barrels down to the speed of the bird, then you must try to get ahead of the bird with just the right amount of lead. Riding the bird out will lead to very inconsistent shooting. Waiting too long to shoot also gives you more time to try and be more precise in turn causing you to aim, not point, which will result in a miss. Another negative to being slow and taking long shots is the increased number of crippled birds as shotguns lose their lethality quickly at a distance. So, what is the right speed? Simply the time it takes to swing, mount, and shoot. Notice I did not say hurry and take a poke, nor did I say mount the gun and chase the bird for a certain distance. Each person as an individual must learn what speed can be executed properly time and again for themselves with one continuous movement. Go shoot your own clays and shoot enough to get a comfortable rhythm, muscle memory will eventually take over. Smooth repetitive shooting builds rhythm, and speed is largely genetic. It took an embarrassing incident to slow me down and to help me become steady to a flush.

Section VI: Another Look at Shooting a Side by Side Properly

A. Factors to Shooting a Side by Side Consistently on Game Birds

5. The Right Focus

When shooting a shotgun, the shot goes where your eyes go because your hand will point where your eyes are looking. That's the single, most important secret to shooting a shotgun. I want you to try a quick little exercise to help make my point. Look at an object 15-20 yards away. Really focus on a certain part of the object, now point your left finger at it quickly. Your left finger will immediately go right to the object with perfect accuracy. You can even close your left eye (if you are right-eye dominate) and check to see if it's perfectly pointing at the object. It will be! How can we point our finger so accurately at an object with no sights or aiming? This is the key to pointing, your eyes are like laser beams and your left hand is the connection to the eyes. If you follow and implement the first four factors I discussed previously, your shotgun will shoot exactly where you look. That is why I wrote this chapter in the order that I did. It is so important to learn to really focus with your eyes on "one" object with intensity. Notice I said one object, this means you cannot look at your barrels! Keep your laser beams locked on the bird's head until you see it crumble and fall. Two common mistakes are to glance at your barrel or sight, or to lift your head up off the stock thinking you can see the bird better. Keep your head down and your face on the stock, and just point your left finger at the bird. Your left hand is holding your barrels, so your barrels are connected to your eyes and left hand.

Practice focusing at clay targets, and even shooting the largest chip left over with your second barrel (this is what I do) as this takes great focus. I'll always tell new shooters to try and miss by shooting in front of the target. In my last book I talked about playing ping pong, tennis, or even going to a batting cage. Think about it, with all three of these sports you must focus with your eyes on the ball (bird) and not your paddle, racket, or bat. That is why athletes with great focus and mind muscle connection can pick up shooting shotguns so well. Go play some sports in the off season with your kids or friends!

In conclusion, I truly believe we can all shoot great if we master and incorporate these five factors to shooting a side by side. All five are important, and some are more important to certain individuals than others. You will learn that all five of these factors work together in tandem to shooting a side by side with consistency on game birds.

Section VI: Another Look at Shooting a Side by Side Properly

B. Handling Shooting Slumps

The dreaded shooting slump, something we all experience sooner or later. Usually there are only a few reasons why we have a slump, now all you have to do is figure out what your own personal reason is for why you're not shooting well.

I have a story that relates perfectly to how a shooting slump can occur instantly. About eight years ago I had a client that had become like family invite me out to his property to shoot some clays. I decided to bring my Parker-Repro 28 gauge because this was the gun I was going to be shooting doves with, in a few weeks. My client and his dad launched target after target, all to be smashed by my 28 gauge. I don't recall ever missing a single clay. I could tell they were both surprised at how well I shot, and they made a comment about how I smashed the clays with a little 28 gauge. A couple months passed by and they invited me to shoot in a sporting clays tournament for their company. I was hesitant because I had never shot sporting clays before, but it sounded like fun. After seeing me shoot my 28 gauge so well at their property they thought having me on their team was an "ace" up their sleeve. I pulled up at the range and pulled out my Fox CE 20 gauge. A I walked around I realized that I was the only person with a side by side. Comments were being made and I started to get nervous. No one could believe I'd bring a side by side 20 gauge, I was out of my element, "totally!" I got coached every time I went to shoot (pre-mount your gun, lead the target, etc.). To make a long story short, I shot terrible. The harder I tried, the worse I shot. I started aiming, looking at my barrels, pre-mounting my gun, trying to make perceived leads. I lost my confidence and was instantly in a shooting slump. I was embarrassed and felt bad for my friends that had faith in me. This was a great lesson for me, and I learned a lot through this experience! I hope my story touched home with a few of you.

"Part Two"

Now for what I do about shooting slumps. First, we must all practice properly swinging and mounting our shotguns over and over to develop muscle memory. You must practice as I talked about in the previous chapters to build great technique and the ability to focus with confidence. Confidence is the key and we all develop confidence in the things that we do regularly. We then become proficient at them.

When I go hunting, I always bring two guns that I shoot well, both having slightly different dimensions. If I shoot poorly on a trip, I do two things when I get back to the lodge. First, I change out my gun, then I swing and mount the gun until my shoulder burns a little. Now I forget about the poor shooting and relax, laugh, and have fun. The next morning, I pull out the new gun and go hunt. I never mount it again or think about anything again. I let my natural instincts kick back in and keep my conscious effort out. I know how to shoot a gun, and I have muscle memory, all I have to do is be confident and enjoy the hunt with no negative distractions. Just relax and focus on the bird, never think about your gun handling! Once you're out hunting it is too late to learn how to handle a gun, this should already be engraved in your mind and body. It's just like riding a bike, just hop on and go!

Some things in life are simply as good as it gets!

Section VII: Hammer Guns "The Iconic Bird Guns"

I have a passion for hammer guns. I know it might sound slightly eccentric but remember that I'm very nostalgic and a true traditionalist. Hammer guns may seem old-fashioned but there's no more elegant firearm than an English hammer gun with a set of graceful swan-necked hammers. A hammer gun's frame and lockplates are smaller than non-hammer guns because they don't have to accommodate large internal tumbles, this reduces weight and creates a slim profile. The hammers can be gracefully sculpted with a pleasing shape and elegant engraving. Add some nicely figured wood, and a set of Damascus barrels with beautiful swirls and you have an iconic bird gun that can bring great pleasure to any gentleman bird hunter.

My fun little hammer .410 getting the job done on doves.

Section VII: Hammer Guns "The Iconic Bird Guns"

A. Timeless Superiorities

After many years of technical advancements, the hammer gun still has some time-honored superiorities over the more modern hammerless gun. First is the simplicity which makes the hammer gun easier to work on, and it is more reliable. With having less parts, the hammer gun will have fewer problems. Secondly, the hammer gun (with rebounding hammers) has a half-cock notch that is automatically engaged and is actually safer than the later trigger-blocking devices of hammerless guns. When the barrels of a hammer gun are closed, and the sears are in the half-cock notch (hammers down), the gun is safe as the gun will not fire when the triggers are pulled or if the gun is even dropped. In contrast, a hammerless gun is fully cocked when closed even though the internal hammers cannot be seen. If a hammer gun is fully cocked and dropped, the gun will not go off. The hammers will fall only part way to the half-cock notch.

My good friend Robert often hunts with a hammer gun.

"Part Two"

Only the most expensive hammerless guns have an intercepting sear to stop the internal hammers from going off. Reliance on a trigger safety is a false sense of security! All hammer guns are considered as easy openers. This is due to the fact that the drop of the barrels do not cock the hammers like on a hammerless gun. Hammer guns by design have a great between-the-hands balance. Hammer guns have a feel of liveliness that no other design of gun has. It's hard to explain, but hammer guns have a different mounting and swinging feel to them. The design allows for longer barrels to be used and still capture a balance that has a low moment of inertia, this can only be described as a sweet feel!

The only real argument that the hammerless gun has as far as a superiority over the hammer gun is that you can fire a hammerless gun faster. We are talking about maybe half a second difference. This should not be a factor at all when shooting over a pointing dog. In some countries the best quality hammer guns are still king in the live pigeon rings where shot gun excellence is self-proving. Keep in mind that two of the most famous game shots used hammer guns clear into the 1920s. These are Lord Ripon and King George V. I'm sure both these gentlemen could out-shoot any of us with our hammerless gun!

Robert's rare Tate 16 gauge hammer gun. What a beauty!

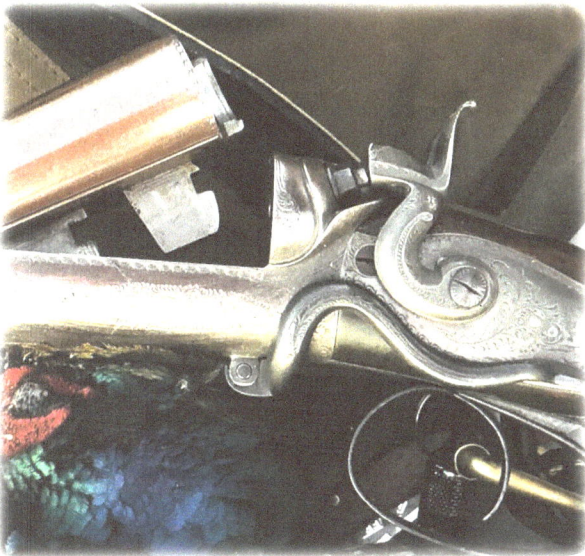

My Perrins and Son. I love this rare left side opener. It's very lively at 5 lbs. 12 oz. The feel of this gun will move you in a special way.

My Boss under-lever hammer 16 gauge. Weighing 5 lbs. 13 oz. This gun has a lively balance that is incomparable to any hammerless gun!

Section VII: Hammer Guns "The Iconic Bird Guns"

B. Damascus Barrels

In my first book, I promised to open the can of worms over Damascus barrels in my next book, so here we go! I love the beautiful time-honored craftsmanship that went into the making of a set of Damascus barrels. The time and skill it took three master barrel makers to make a set of Damascus barrels is mind boggling in today's automated machine era. The beauty is captivating to true traditionalists that are nostalgic. The beauty of Damascus barrels is not only skin deep, they are equally usable as modern steel barrels!

This Parker has Bernard Damascus barrels that have a very distinct pattern.

I regularly shoot three different guns that have Damascus barrels. Over the years I have owned and hunted with well over fifteen different guns made with Damascus barrels. My conclusions come from experience and research. Over the years, I have learned a lot from some of the best gunsmiths and gun makers. Let me try to explain my position on Damascus barrels. Right off I want to make a note that I am not referring to low quality Damascus that was used in inexpensive trade guns that were imported by various manufacturers. Believe me when I say that there were an equal number of guns going around with cheap inferior steel barrels!

My LeFever is a perfect example of fine English Damascus.

Quality is quality; let's compare apples to apples. In 1888, the Birmingham Proof House made an exhaustive test comparison of steel and Damascus barrels, which proved conclusively that there was no technical superiority to be found between best English Damascus and best English gun-barrel steel. If a set of barrels are in current nitro proof, you can safely use Damascus or steel barrels with the loads they were proofed for, period. Let me give an example: my Perrins & Son hammer 16 gauge has the following stamps on the barrel flats: Proof 77, (BNP) 2 1/2", 1 oz., and .667. What the stamps mean is that the barrels were nitro proofed in 1977 for 2 1/2 shells loaded with a maximum of 1 oz. of shot. The bores had a measurement of .667 when they were deemed safe in the proof house. When I bought the gun the bores still measured .667 and the chambers were still 2 1/2", the gun is still in proof. As we should do with any set of barrels, I had them inspected for any rust or pitting of any kind, dents or bulges, loose ribs, and minimum barrel wall thickness. As with all English barrels, whether they are Damascus or steel, they are in proof and safe, or they are out of proof and not guaranteed safe; end of story! With any shotgun, use the ammunition that the gun is designed to shoot. At one time, I owned a best quality Stephen Grant hammer gun with best quality Damascus barrels. The gun would shoot the nicest even patterns one could imagine. All my high-quality English guns having Damascus barrels seemed to pattern fantastic. I started to believe that Damascus was somehow superior to steel barrels. I now realize an English best is an English best! (apples to apples)

The barrels do have some differences. The differences have nothing to do with quality or superiority. I will not bore you with how Damascus barrels are made beyond that they are made by twisting strands of steel and iron that are welded together, then winded around a mandrel while hot, hammer foraging them. This is a very hard, time-consuming process that usually takes three skilled barrel makers to make a set of

"Part Two"

Damascus barrels. Now for the inherent differences. The fact that Damascus is designed from using steel and iron, steel barrels will be harder because iron is softer than steel and the advancements in modern metallurgy in steel is amazing. Barrels only need to be a certain hardness and making them harder only helps prevent denting from misuse and carelessness. Damascus is more prone to rust, so proper cleaning and storage is a must. When a shotgun is fired, a pressure wave goes through the bores and stretches them. All barrels must be elastic enough to be restored to the proper size after the pressure wave passes. Damascus barrels do this better than harder steel barrels. The hands-on craftsmanship required to make a set of best Damascus barrels usually results in very precise measurements in the bores and the concentricity. Look at a high-quality set of Damascus barrels and you will see the nice taper from the chambers to the muzzles, and you can also feel how the weight is in the chambers and not in the muzzles.

Many countries have produced high quality Damascus. England is usually mentioned first, but Belgium's best is just as good. My Parker has Bernard Damascus barrels, they are high quality and from France. Some lower quality Damascus went around from Belgium and Spain, but this was on cheap, low cost boxlocks. After all my research, I am convinced that the demise of Damascus was primarily due to the cost of making a set of Damascus barrels. Steel barrels were more practical and saved a lot of time and money. Keep in mind that when nitro powder first came onto the scene, cartridges were loaded to much lower pressures than today's 2 3/4-inch loads of dynamite. The ever-popular load for the English 12 gauge was 2 1/2-inch with 1 1/16 oz. of shot. All these loads produced between 6,500 – 7,500 PSI of pressure, not a problem for Damascus!

I would love to see every fellow gentleman of the uplands get a chance to own at least one good hammer gun with Damascus barrels. You can get a high-quality English best hammer gun with Damascus barrels for about half the cost of the same equivalent without hammers and steel barrels. In the back of my book, I listed some reputable dealers that can make sure your Damascus barrels are in proof and safe to shoot with the right ammunition. Now that the cat's out of the bag, and someone was willing to objectively discuss Damascus barrels, the cost of a fine double with Damascus barrels will probably go up, so go find one soon and enjoy the beautiful craftsmanship of a fine pair of Damascus barrels that reflect a time of hard work and perfection when the almighty dollar was not number one.

English best guns represent the finest in craftsmanship and have impeccable balance. The graceful lines and artistry they display are incomparable!

Section VIII: English Best Side by Sides

Handmade Best Gun

Well, in the last two chapters I'm sure I stirred up some controversy that I'll hear about, so let's throw some more coal on the fire with this chapter. In my first book, I very briefly said that I felt that the English made the best side by sides in the world and this is my stance as I always promise to be honest and straight forward. I think it is fitting that I should thoroughly explain why I have this opinion as well as explain the differences between a handmade English best gun and a machine-made double. Put your seat belt on as you read this chapter, we are going for a ride to England.

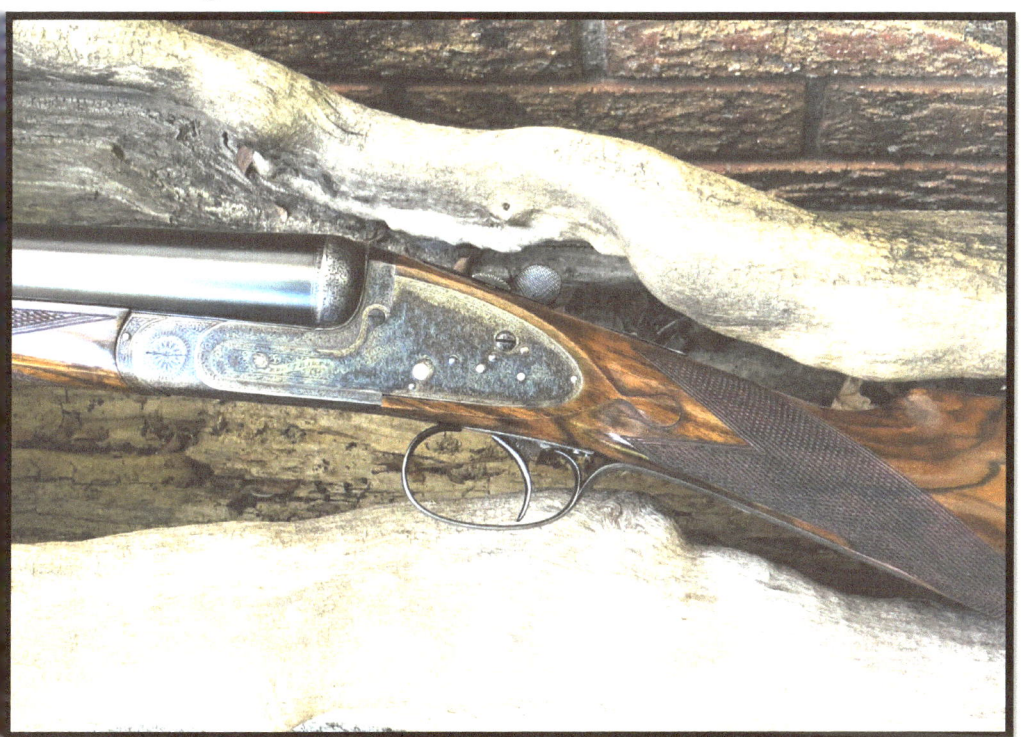

My Fredrick T-Baker is a great example of a English best sidelock. This classy gun weighs 6 lbs 5 oz and handles like a dream.

In England there are too many makers that made a best quality double to mention them all, so I'll talk about four makers from London that only made best guns: Purdey, Grant, Woodward and Boss. These guns are designed to be lightweight game guns, solely with the purpose to shoot game birds, not clay pigeons or any other type of animal. The other purpose of a London best is to have a gun that is refined and finished to the highest degree as humanly possible, with no money restrictions, just pure perfection.

My E.J. Churchill boxlock is an example of an English best boxlock.

My Arthur Hill is an example of an English best sidelock that is a pure upland delight.

My Bentley and Playfair is an example of a side plated boxlock English best.

The Traditional Side by Side

"Part Two"

A gun that has unmatched balance and handling qualities, to aid in natural shooting, and bring out the shooter's skill to their highest personal level. All English best are made to last for generations if properly cared for. Once you have handled and shot an English best, you will know the difference between a handmade best gun and a machine-made gun. Now, for a Doug Stewart analogy. When I was 16 years old, I bought a 1969 Ford Mustang. The car had a 351 V-8 engine that I rebuilt with a Holly 4-barrel carb, Headman headers, a dual point distributor, etc. This was my fast sports car. The car would lay rubber like no other as it would suck you back in the seat for a thrill ride. This was not the only thrill the car produced! The brakes were so poor that you had to plan your stops well in advance. You also had to take any bump in the road real slow or the front end would bottom out and knock your teeth out. The car was a handful driving up canyons, and the steering helped to develop my first arm muscles. Between the loud engine and wind noise blowing through the poor sealed windows, you could forget about listening to the old A.M. radio or a passenger talking to you. The doors were so hard to shut that I had one fly open on me once going around a corner. The car was cold blooded and hard to start, cold in the winter, and hot in the summer. I thought all this was normal, the way a sports car should be. About fifteen years later, I had a very wealthy client purchase a Lamborghini. This car cost as much as my house and was awe-inspiring. My client took me for a ride in the Lamborghini up the canyon. This car was fast, smooth, and went around the curves in the canyon like the tires were glued to the road. The car would stop on a dime. The car was more stable at 100 miles per hour than my mustang was driving through a school zone. This car was refined to the point of perfection, at any cost. Both cars could get you from point A to point B, and both are good at picking up chicks. Off hand, these are the only similarities I could think of. I know that the American made Mustang has come a long way since 1969 but it is still no match for the Lamborghini that would go 230 miles an hour and with every single little part made to perfection, without any corners being cut in manufacturing to lower costs. This is quite the analogy, but I think it makes my point.

An English best is not a best gun because it has one or two great features, it takes the sum of all parts to be a best gun. Let's talk about the stock of the gun first. A best gun will have a French walnut stock. French walnut is very durable, this is important at the head of the stock, and in general for hard use against different weather conditions, or even just being banged around. French walnut has been proven to be one of the most stable woods against shrinking or cracking from humidity changes, temperature changes, or when the stock blanks are being worked into shape. French walnut is undeniably beautiful, and light weight, yet strong, a perfect choice for a lightweight game gun. Last, but not least, French walnut is scarce and very expensive. Now that we know the best wood available is used to make the stock, the best craftsmen have the perfect platform to design a stock precise in size, shape, and weight. If the gun was ordered to weigh 6 1/2 lbs., a stock blank with a certain weight is picked. This is important for a well-balanced gun. A mass-produced machine-made gun will have a stock with almost any weight variation. Once the gun is completed, the stock will often be hollowed out, or have lead added to the end of the stock. This is the wrong way to change the balance point on a game gun! A big weight change in a small section of a gun at either end (the barrels or stock) will cause a strange clumsy feel to the entire gun from poor weight distribution. The checkering is sharp to prevent hand slippage, with the points all being even with no run-ons. The checkering on a best gun is handsome and perfect but meant for function. Overly fine elaborate checkering can look gaudy and fails as a nonslip surface under recoil and gun handling. The stocker must fit the stock to the action so precise that the wood and steel look as if they have grown together. The sleek stock that is made to the exact measurements requested is sanded to the smoothest surface imaginable. A special stain and sealing ingredient are applied to the stock. Their own special oil mixture is hand rubbed in, little by little, coat after coat. This is done at daily intervals for up to six weeks. When the finish is done not a single pore in the wood will be showing. This stock will last forever if properly taken care of. The stock will be impenetrable from rain or sun. Any wear marks can easily be fixed with a drop of boiled linseed oil.

The sidelock is the action of choice for an English best. This is the English's choice of action for a few reasons. The lengthy configuration of a sidelock action has a better distribution of weight than a boxlock action. The action bar of a sidelock is solid and strong, and in turn, the entire action is smaller and graceful. With the action body being thinner the head of the stock is smaller with an elegant appearance. All the interior parts are perfectly fitted, and hand filed to perfection. No machine can cut and sculpt complex parts like a man with a file and a stone. The trigger pulls will be crisp with the exact weight of pull that was requested. All the parts will be hand polished to such a high degree that rust or any other type of corrosion cannot find a pore in the steel to stick to. Some English best go a step further and gold plate the internal parts. You can take the locks out of an English best that is over 100 years old and they will look like they were made yesterday. This takes a highly skilled craftsman to construct and regulate the technical sidelock with all its individual parts. This is highly time consuming and costly.

Now the barrels, which I like to call the heart of the gun. I'll discuss the fine steel barrels on an English best since I already have written about fine Damascus barrels. First off, the barrels are made from the finest steels available to achieve hardness and strength, light weight, and elasticity. The barrels will be thin and tapered with a beautiful swooping profile. Most American guns have overly thick heavy barrels that make long barreled guns feel sluggish and poorly balanced. Long barreled English guns can feel light and responsive with an elegant look. On an English best the barrels will get thinner past the midpoint, but the bores will be consistent to within .001 an inch from the forcing cones to the choke section. Usually a lightweight game gun will have 2 1/2-inch chambers and is built to weigh between 6 1/4 to 6 3/4 lbs. for a standard 12 gauge unless ordered differently. The bores will be polished as smooth as glass and cut with perfect concentricity. The choke section is usually as long as the shot charge that is going to be fired through the gun. The choke section will be perfectly concentric with the bores and cut in a conical-parallel style. Usually American guns will have just a conical choke with no parallel section, as the parallel section is hard to properly cut and regulate. The barrels will be regulated to hit the point of aim perfectly at 40 yards. This process is called "Englishing" the gun. The barrels will print a perfect pattern, to the exact percentage requested by the buyer at 40 yards with the prescribed load. For example, say the customer wanted the gun to put a 1 1/16 oz. load of number 7 shot, 60% above the target at 40 yards, and 40% of the load below the center of the target. Now let's say the customer wanted 50% of his pattern in the 30" circle at 40 yards out of the right barrel, and 65% in the 30" circle out of his left barrel. This customer will get exactly what he ordered! Now for a best English finish. The barrels are struck up using striking irons. The barrels are then polished by hand with emery cloth until the barrels are so smooth that a single strike mark cannot be seen. This process can take up to one week. A factory-made gun will have visible strike marks, and a wavy surface that is not smooth nor polished. The ugly mass-produced gun barrels will be dipped in a liquid chemical bath that colors the steel and produces a wavy finish called bluing. Best guns use a process called blacking.

"Part Two"

This is a time-consuming process that allows the barrels to rust, be cleaned, re-rusted, and re-cleaned over and over. When the right color is achieved the process is over. This process can take two weeks, but will produce a deep, even color than can last virtually forever.

After reviewing the process in the making of an English best game gun I hope you can see why I think they are the best guns made, with the most refinement. These guns are made the old-world way, in the purest form possible. Why would anyone need a gun that is so great? Why do people need million-dollar homes, fancy boats, expensive jewelry, expensive shoes, the best golf clubs, etc.? I guess sometimes people are so passionate about something that they want the very best, and appreciate the incredible art that man is capable of producing in a new, modern, automated world.

Be proud and true to your heritage.

Section IX: The Great American Side by Sides

After reading the last chapter you might draw the conclusion that I only like English best shotguns, but this is not the case. I own and shoot American made side by sides more than any other make of shotgun. I'm proud to be an American, and I'm proud of our forefather's craftsmanship. I think it is special that Americans came up with their own unique design for side by side shotguns. Many countries just copy the English best. The Spanish and Italians come to my mind immediately with their best sidelocks. Now, let's look at an American made Parker. When I see a painting of a hunter in the woods flushing a grouse over the point of his setter and shooting a Parker side by side, it moves me. I'm nostalgic and love to shoot the guns that our forefathers shot in the uplands of North America. I don't need the world's best. I shoot American made side by sides as good as any gun, if they fit me. It is amazing how well Americans made shotguns prior to the war with mostly machines. Hand work was still involved where it really mattered. Pre-war American made side by sides were not the best in the world, but darn close in the higher grades, with incredible reliability. Americans took great pride in checkering. Highly figured wood and fine elaborate checkering was a trademark on high grade American doubles. The English checkered their guns for function with a simpler, more-coarse pattern. High grade American doubles also had game scenes engraved in them, sometimes to the point of being gaudy. I like a setter or maybe a quail scene on my bird gun. It's all a matter of personal taste. Hunting Bob White quail in the South is one of Americas richest traditions and should be hunted with a lightweight American made side by side. This is pure harmony. The majority of American made side by sides are heavy guns that were made to be reliable and capable of shooting heavy loads at many different types of animals. But if you look hard enough as I have done, you can find light weight, well-balanced bird guns.

The Traditional Side by Side

"Part Two"

In this section I'm going to give my opinion of some American doubles that I have owned. I'll stick to the American made side by sides and my own personal experiences owning and shooting these guns. I think by the end of this section of my book, you will realize that the only logical thing to do is to own an English best and an American best side by side!

Section IX: The Great American Side by Sides

A. Parker "Old Reliable"

Parkers are probably the most sought after and collectable American made side by side. After reading my first book you'll know that Parkers are my favorite American made side by side. I search and find the lightweight Parkers for my upland gunning. Most Parkers are heavy guns and are not light enough to be ideal bird guns that can be carried for endless miles. My choice Parkers are the 12 gauges built on a 1 frame with 26" barrels, 0 frame 16 gauges, 0 frame 20 gauges, and 00 frame 28 gauges. From the 12 gauge to the 28 gauge, the weights I look for vary from 6 3/4 lbs. for the 12 gauges to 5 1/2 lbs. for the 28 gauges. The 16 gauges built on a 0 frame that weigh approximately 6 lbs. are my favorite.

This is my all original Parker VHE 00 frame 28 gauge.

"Part Two"

I feel that Parkers have a better balance to them than any other American made side by side. I know there are exceptions to this rule, but nine times out of ten the Parker is balanced better than other American made side by sides. Parkers have a way of feeling much lighter than they actually are. Parkers have great balance between your hands which naturally lends the gun to instinctive wing shooting. This is especially true with lightweight Parkers that have 26" barrels. From the beginning, Parkers were built with a great balance to them. The balance point was always important in the production of Parkers. I also believe that the great balance of a Parker shotgun was accidently inherited by the design of the tall frame that is heavy and narrow. This puts a vast majority of the gun weight close to the trigger hand. When someone tells you that they could not shoot a Parker well it is usually because of the poor stock fit, as older Parkers usually had short stocks with a lot of drop. When I buy a Parker, the gun must have a length of pull that fits me and the drop needs to be close enough to my dimensions so I can have the stock bent a little to fit me perfectly. I never add a pad to a factory original Parker because this will add three ounces to the back of the gun and ruin the balance. Most people will find that if they shoot a Parker that fits them, they will shoot amazingly well. Parkers are tough, reliable guns that have great regulated barrels and good triggers. The old-school design is very eye catching and they have a distinctively different look to them than other side by sides. I'm not sure exactly how Parkers became cult status, but I'm sure the fact that Parker had massive advertising campaigns and that thousands of Parkers were made in the golden pre-world war era of American shotgunning helped. All I know is that Charles Parker set out to build the sportsmen of America a better gun and did just that!

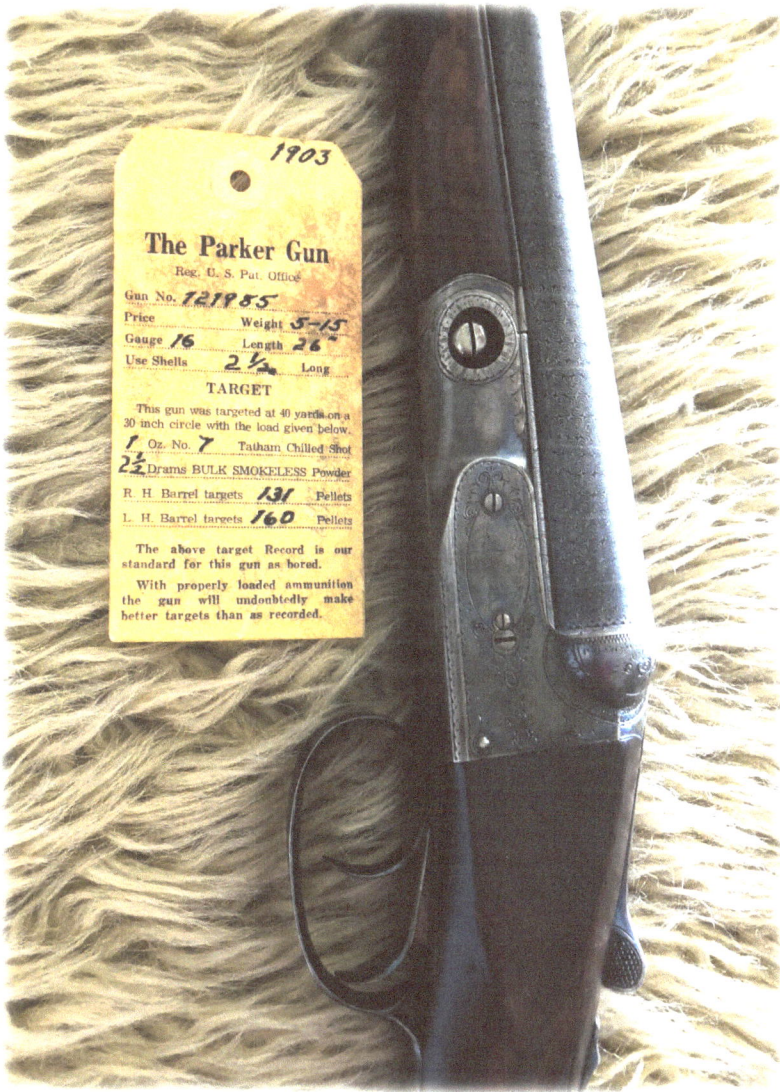

My all original Parker 0 frame GH 16 gauge.

Section IX: The Great American Side by Sides

B. A.H. Fox "The Finest Gun in the World"

The great A.H. Fox. I still ride the struggle bus between Parkers and Foxes! How can someone not appreciate the design of a Fox? One of the Fox's greatest attributes is the simple design that the Fox has. This durable gun is made with fewer parts than any other American made side by side. The simplicity makes the Fox easy to work on and very reliable. I have found that most of the 12 gauges are heavy and not balanced about the hinge pin. The best balanced 12 gauges for the uplands have the number 4 lightweight barrels 26" in length. The 16 gauges and 20 gauges with number 4 weight barrels are light weight with great balance for the uplands. The small bores are built on a small 20 gauge frame. Small-bore Foxes have one of the most elegant properly proportioned frames of any boxlock action made in the world. I think the small-bore Fox was Ansley's greatest achievement. The 16 gauge on the tiny 20 gauge frame moves me in a special way, a way that makes me proud of an American invention. Tony Galazan agrees with me and resurrected the great small-bore Foxes. I ordered a Fox CE 20 gauge (my favorite grade) shortly after Tony started making them. My Fox has 29" barrels and weighs 5 lbs. 9 ounces. This is a great upland bird gun. Foxes are known to be reliable guns and they have a great single trigger design that works well. The barrels are excellent quality along with an action that wears in and stays tight. I personally have never been able to shoot the heavier 12 gauge Foxes as well as Parkers, but the small-bore Foxes seem to handle great for me. Original small-bore Foxes have become quite collectable. Fox's are great guns and should be on any side by side enthusiast's list of best made American doubles.

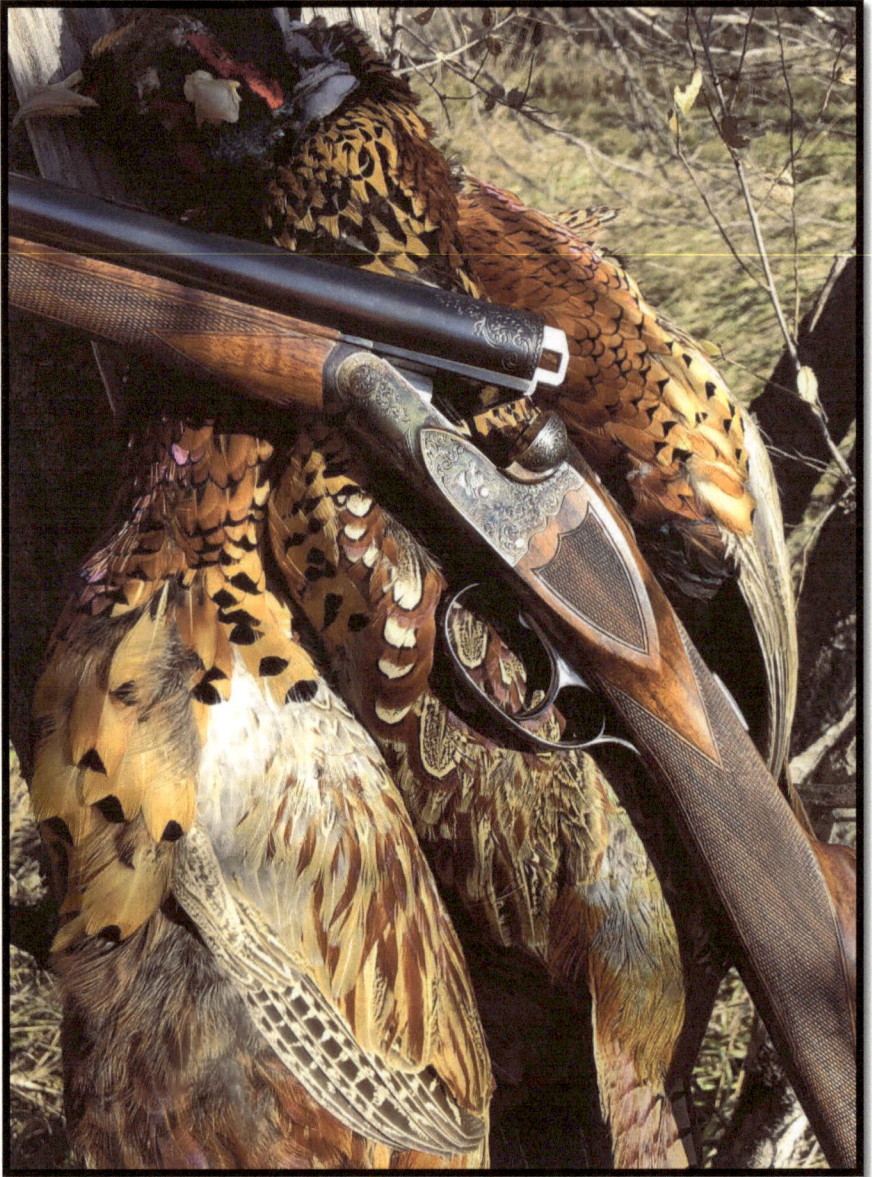

My custom ordered Fox CE 20 gauge. A delight at 5 lbs 9 oz.

This is the one and only Double Gun Journal. It is like Christmas when I get my issue. Every side by side enthusiast should subscribe to this invaluable resource on doubles. I have learned much over the years from Daniel Cote's excellent magazine and Daniel is a good man that loves doubles.

Call to subscribe (231)-536-7439.

Section IX: The Great American Side by Sides

C. LeFever "Uncle Dan's"

The wonderful LeFever was a very advanced side by side well ahead of any other American made side by side. A LeFever is completely adjustable, to the point that every part of the action can be adjusted with a simple screwdriver to compensate for wear. Many older doubles will get loose on the hinge pin. The LeFever's barrels pivot on a ball and socket instead of a conventional hinge pin and can be tightened by seating the screw deeper. The cocking system on LeFevers makes the gun easy to open and has other functions such as nudging fired cartridges forward. LeFevers had great barrels, triggers, and stocks. I've only owned three LeFevers over the years and wish I still had them all. The gems are the Automatic Hammerless guns and the D.M. LeFevers. The design of the LeFever is genius and different than other doubles in a good way. The high-grade top-of-the-line LeFevers such as the Optimus Grade is a truly magnificent gun that could rival any Parker! The problem is that people don't sell their LeFevers and that very few were made for a short period of time. If you actually find a graded LeFever in excellent original condition, expect to pay a lot of money. Find a LeFever 16 gauge with a XX stamped on the water table and you will have a legendary upland bird gun!

I now own this fine original LeFever H 20 gauge. At 5 lbs. 14 oz it handles like an extension of your arm. Small bore LeFever's are rare little jewels.

I finally got my dream gun as I was writing this book. Thanks to
Daniel Cote I now own this fine LeFever FE 16 gauge.

Section IX: The Great American Side by Sides

D. L.C. Smith "Sweet Elsie"

Many years ago, I decided that I just had to own a L.C. Smith. I had already owned a Parker, Fox and Winchester, but not a L.C. Smith. I knew that a lightweight 16 gauge was in order. I called the L.C. Smith man named Walt Schiessl. I told him that I was looking for a lightweight 16 gauge with a straight stock. Walt told me that straight stocked L.C. Smiths are rare and that I could be waiting quite a while. My mind was made up and I was willing to wait! Walt was a real nice man and promised to call me if he found one. After what seemed like an eternity, I got my phone call. Walt was excited and said, "Son, I found your perfect bird gun." It was a lightweight 16 gauge model 3E with 28" barrels, a straight stalk, and a single trigger with no safety. The little Smith weighed 6 lbs. and was stocked with a beautiful piece of fiddleback walnut. Walt was right, this has been one of the best bird guns of all time. This L.C. Smith is on the front cover of my first book with a pheasant, two Bob White quail, and a prairie chicken.

This is my famous L.C. Smith 3E 16 gauge that graced the cover of my first book and has been a great hunting companion of mine for decades.

Now for the breakdown on L.C. Smiths. My model 3E 16 gauge was built in 1908. The pre-1913 L.C. Smiths are a different breed of gun than the post-war guns. I learned this the hard way. The pre-war L.C. Smiths have gracefully filed frames, the fences are sculpted in a pleasing manner, the stocks are trimmer with finer checkering, and the entire fit and finish is superior. My Smith has a great functioning single trigger, and no cracks behind the side plates. I took the side plates off and was pleased to see the insides nicely polished and fitted in the wood. I loved L.C. Smiths and bought gun after gun. After owning too many different L.C. Smiths to count, I came to some new conclusions. Most L.C. Smiths were heavy guns and poorly balanced. The best bets were feather weights with 26" barrels. I have had bad luck with hunter single triggers, I guess I just got lucky with my 3E 16 gauge. When you take the locks out of the post-war Smiths, you will see file marks everywhere and the machine cutouts for the lock work and the entire head of the stock is crude. The post-war guns used hard American walnut for their stocks, and the lockplates are milled square at the edges and not beveled toward the inside. This combination contributes to the stock to split at the rear of the side plates. I had to have a few Smiths undercut around the rear of the plates by my Uncle Mike to prevent the splitting. L.C. Smiths have a great top fastener, and are hard to shoot loose, but in general I feel that L.C. Smiths are a little more unreliable than other American made doubles and not as graceful as English sidelocks.

With all this said, I found a diamond in the rough and love my old L.C. Smith. The hunt for a great L.C. Smith can land you with a jewel for life!

Section IX: The Great American Side by Sides

E. Winchester Model 21 "The Resilient American Classic"

The Model 21 came to life in the great depression and still survives today. This is quite a feat, showing strong American resilience. If a gun's strength and durability is of top priority to you, then a Model 21 should be on the top of your list of guns to own. John Olin was a great privateer that set out to build a strong gun and he was smart to promote the incredible strength it had. I have owned several Model 21's and have had zero problems with them. Their single trigger is probably one of the best single triggers ever made on an American double. The barrels are well bored, and the guns have good pointability. The Model 21 was a great design for the famous trap model. I also like the short opening radius that the Model 21 has.

I regretfully sold this gun. My Model 21 16 gauge screamed American made!

"Part Two"

Now for the negatives. I only like and shoot lightweight bird guns that have a hinge pin balance or a balance even closer to the trigger hand. The Model 21 is a heavy gun and not balanced to suit me. The frames are long and heavy. With the long and heavy action bar, the weight is distributed far out towards the barrels. Model 21's feel awkward to me when I swing them and are uncomfortable to carry for miles on end. I found a few 20 gauges with a straight stock and 26" barrels that weren't too bad, but they still weighed 6 1/2 pounds. The 28 gauge and .410 bores are even worse, as they are built on 20 gauge frames and weigh even more. I can't deny that most Model 21's have beautifully figured wood, and that Winchester designed the most attractive beaver tail forearm of all America doubles, but the plain, blued frame does nothing for me.

With all the good, bad, and ugly, the Model 21 is a true American survivor that represents strength and resilience.

Section IX: The Great American Side by Sides

F. ITHACA "The Simple Wonder"

The Ithaca has a great simple design that utilizes few parts like the Fox. The design is thoughtful and strong. The action has a tight lock up that stays tight. As for the triggers, they are ugly, have an odd shape and are placed too close together. But I must say that the triggers are reliable with a good crisp pull and seem to keep their adjustment. Ithaca's have always been reliable guns at a more affordable price than the other American doubles. To my eye, Ithaca's are not as attractive as other American doubles and not quite as meticulously designed in general. Beauty is only skin deep, and a lightweight Ithaca can make a great bird gun. I have an Ithaca Flues model 3E 28 gauge. This little gun weighs 5lbs. 7 oz. and has great balance. The engraving is crude, but the checkering and the figure in the wood are dynamite. The 28 gauge is built on a true 28 gauge frame (15/16 of an inch between the firing pin centers) and has nice barrels that taper to the muzzles. This little gun is a woodcock and grouse hunter's jewel at a fraction of the cost of a Parker 28 gauge!

The Ithaca could be the sleeper of all the American doubles out there. Many Ithaca's are heavy with poor balance, but lightweight Ithaca's that have a great between the hands balance are out there. Look patiently and quietly to keep the secret of the great affordable American wonder.

This is my Ithaca 3E 28 gauge. A true upland 28 gauge that has a properly scaled frame weigh
lbs 7 oz.

True collectors are gentlemen that have a higher level of passion, appreciation, and understanding for the item they are collecting.

Section X: Gun Collecting

I appreciate many different side by sides and will always own a variety of different makes, models, and gauges. I'm more of a shotgun accumulator than a collector. Parkers are the only side by sides that I collect. Currently, I own seven original Parkers and three reproductions. I am always in the market to add a Parker to my collection. Personally, I have had the most success buying and selling American made side by sides.

By buying a good gun at a fair price and upselling my guns at the right time has resulted in my current collection. No one knows everything about every gun! I suggest you stick with one manufacturer and become as educated as you can about that gun maker and their guns. Gun prices are out of control and the economy is very unstable. Do not plan on making a lot of money, the good old days are gone, and you must collect more for the love of your favorite side by side than for a profit. I'm going to share with you the things I've learned about collecting Parkers as I feel that my advice can be applied to collecting most side by sides!

First, you need to figure out exactly the gun you're looking for. For example, I collect only lightweight Parkers that fit me, and make great upland bird guns. I'm rich in life, God has blessed me with great happiness, but I'm not rich financially. I must buy guns that I can turn around tomorrow and sell if my family needs the money. So, I must make great deals and buy desirable guns that most people can afford and want to own. This takes great patience with a lot of looking, and usually disqualifies most dealers. Dealers need to make money, so their prices are most often astronomical. Now there is a whole other breed of collectors that will pay almost anything to get what they want. This breed of collectors uses certain dealers and usually have the best collections. Personally, I'm okay with not having deep pockets. I think that the hunt is half the fun of collecting and I appreciate and enjoy every gun I collect. I take great care of my guns, and I shoot and enjoy them all!

Now that you have narrowed down the type of gun that you want to collect and why, it's time to educate yourself about this gun. When I decided that Parkers were the guns that I wanted to collect, I bought every available book on Parkers. I got to know some great Parker dealers like Herschel Chadick and some great Parker restorators. I joined the Parkers Gun Collectors Association and befriended Parker collectors and researched the guns in every way I possibly could. I have a very complete library on Parkers with articles and my own research. The bottom line is that I had to become my own expert on Parkers and not just take other people's word about them.

Cash is king when collecting side by sides. When you trade a gun in on another gun, you'll be getting less money on your gun. It is usually better to sell your gun out right. I have had good luck selling my guns off Guns International, and even better luck selling my guns off the Parker site. Dealers will sell your guns for you, but with a 15% commission. I'm not one to haggle over price, but if you are willing to pay cash, most people will drop the asking price a little.

The most collectable guns will be in excellent original condition, not restored. It is better to have a lower grade Parker like a VH in original condition with good dimensions, unturned screws, butt plate, 80% plus case colors, 90% blue, tight on face, and completely unaltered from the original factory order than it is to have a higher grade Parker like a DH that is not all original with damaged screws, no case colors, 3 inches of drop, and a length of pull at 13 1/2 inches. Rare Parkers that were made in small quantities bring the most money if the dimensions of the gun are desirable and the condition is good. For example, all 28 gauge Parkers are rare, but a 28 gauge on a 00 frame with 28 inch barrels and a straight stalk with a 14 1/4-inch pull and in great condition is rare and desirable. Now let's take a 28 gauge on a 0 frame with 32-inch barrels and a round knob stalk with a 13 1/2-inch pull and in great condition. This gun is rarer than the first gun, but with less desirable dimensions and would be harder to sell. Also, remember that quality is more important than quantity, as a few really good guns are better to own than to own a bunch of mediocre guns. Recently I sold an excellent benchmark Parker that any Parker collector could appreciate. The gun was a late Remington Parker VHE 16 gauge on a number 1 frame. The gun had 26-inch barrels, and a straight stock with great figure in the wood and with good shooting dimensions. I determined the gun to be all original and in excellent, almost new condition. The case colors were at 97% and were real Remington colors with an appropriate amount of related patina to them. All the screws were in perfect unturned condition, and the gun was tight as new. The barrel bluing was the correct dark blue with sharp lettering and just the right amount of age-related thinning where they were held. The trigger guard blue was correctly a lighter blue that is shinier, to where you can see your reflection in it, but duller and thinner where you hand-held the gun. The checkering was correct and not re-cut, it was properly, slightly dulled and darkened in. Even the oil finish was the correct type of oil and just starting to craze a little. The age-related slight wear was all proper, correlating to each other, and all the finishes were Remington correct. I looked and found the serial number in the stock under the trigger guard. And, just to sleep soundly, I called every gun restorator that I thought could be capable of this perfect work, and the gun was in no ones' records. This Parker did not have a letter on it, but as I mentioned earlier, I did my homework and am confident that this gun was original. I sold this gun because it was 6 lbs. 13 ounces and not a lightweight Parker. If this gun was a 16 gauge on an O frame and weighed 6 lbs. it would still be in my gun cabinet. I traded the gun for an E.J. Churchill Hercules XXV.

The Parker is probably worth more and will keep going up in value. I guess my gun accumulator side kicked in. But in the long run I got a great bird gun in the Churchill, and I stuck to my guns on what I collect, rare lightweight Parkers!

The scars of time define a gun's true charm.

Section XI: Buying a Used Side by Side

If you buy a side by side, you will more than likely buy a used gun that was made a long time ago. A new Bespoken side by side can still be purchased in our country from Connecticut Shotgun Manufacturing Company, or you can order one from another country. In this case, all you have to do is figure out how you want the gun to be made, and how to pay for it. Most of us will buy used side by sides that have traveled the country and have killed birds in the uplands for decades. These guns will have scars from the many adventures, and if they are in good working order, they will be ready for more adventures in the uplands. In the last chapter, I gave some advice on gun collecting and, in this chapter, I'll teach you what to look for to make sure you're getting a good, safe, working side by side for hunting the uplands.

I like to see the guns that I buy in person. This is becoming harder and harder nowadays. I personally cannot travel the country going to gun shows. The local gun shows here in Colorado where I live seem to sell nothing but assault weapons and handguns. When the collector shows come, all the guns are over-priced. Like many of you, I now buy most of my guns off the internet. I routinely use five or six different gun dealers that I trust and respect. Gun dealers charge more than individuals, but they are experts and have the tools to give me very precise measurements and dimensions that I request. I'm not one to haggle over price, out of respect I will ask if there is any room in the price, period. Never argue with a dealer, take the high road and move on. I'm thankful that there are dealers in fine side by sides! Being an honorable gentleman will get you far. Many a dealer has worked trades with me, consigned my guns for me, worked layaway plans, and have given me discounts. Every businessman should want to have a good reputation and have loyal customers. I also like the reassurance that I can return the gun if I'm not satisfied. The

"Part Two"

dealers that I use know that I will return the gun for a full refund if the gun is not exactly as described. All this is worth paying more to me and I like supporting dealers. Sure, I'll buy a gun from a friend once in a while, but not on a regular basis. On even a rarer occasion, I'll buy a gun at a gun show.

Once I have looked over the gun's pictures a million times on the internet and have decided the price is close to what I'm willing to spend, only then will I make a call for the Doug Stewart shake down. I always start my questions with the barrels first. The barrels are the heart of the gun and if the barrels are bad there is no saving the gun. I ask for the length and if they have ever been cut. Barrels that have been cut may not shoot to the point of aim, and the choke section is shortened. More often than not, barrels should touch at the muzzle. Depending on the style of ribs, keels should be present. A raised rib like a Churchill rib will not have keels, but most styles will. Next, I ask how long the choke section is, what style are the chokes cut in, and what the actual chokes are in thousandths of an inch. I even ask if the chokes look like they are concentric. This can all tell me a lot on how the gun is going to pattern. I personally do not want a set of barrels that have any dents or bulges, so this is my next question. What is the bore diameter, and how consistent is that measurement down the length of the bore? This will tell me if the bores have been polished or over-bored. The consistency of the measurement will let me know how professional the job was done. The chamber length is important, and it is also important that the barrels are nitro-proofed if the gun was made outside of the United States. I have the dealer hang the barrels on an index finger off the lump. Then I have them take their other hand and tap the outside of the barrels with the back of their fingernail from top to bottom. The barrels should ring true like a church bell. Another method is to lightly tap the top of the rib with a rubber mallet while a fingernail is dragged down the rib next to the barrel and mallet. The vibration should be consistent. Large sections of a hollow thud without a vibration is not good. Mind you that both these methods are not full proof. Many a great gun has been passed up thinking the ribs are loose. Often there is enough gaps between the soldering that the barrels will not ring well. The only true test is to dunk the barrels in a tank, air bubbles don't lie. The dealer won't dunk the barrels, but if they ring well you can move on with the questions. Now I want to know what the minimum barrel wall thickness is. The British gun trade has no set standard, as long as the barrels pass a proof test, they are deemed safe. English guns should be shot with the proper loads that the gun was made to shoot. All the needed stamping will be on the barrel flats. I go by a general excepted English standard. This is a minimum wall thickness of .020 inch for shotguns chambered for 2 1/2-inch shells, and a minimum wall thickness of .025 inch for shotguns chambered for 2 3/4-inch shells. American made shotguns are usually over built and can measure .035 inch or more. I shoot low pressure ammo, so the English standard is great for me. Minimum wall thickness is important, and dealers use a wall thickness micrometer for a precise measurement. Now I ask if the bores have any rust or pitting, often perfect bores are referred to as having mirror bores. A little bit of hazing is okay as long as the hazing spot is smooth. Make sure the dealer checks the ejectors if the gun has them, you want everything working right. The last thing I ask about the barrels is if they have been re-blued.

Once I am happy with the barrels, it's time to evaluate the rest of the gun. I only buy guns with the stock dimensions that I need to shoot well, unless I'm just collecting the gun. If all the stock dimensions are not listed in the ad, I'll ask for them. Then I ask how much the gun weighs and where the balance point is. The stock must not have any cracks or be poorly fitted to the receiver. I have the dealer look closely by the tang, behind the receiver (side plates), around the trigger guard, and through the wrist area. If the stock is poorly fitted, it could be a stock replacement. Personally, I do not like stock replacements. I ask the dealer to fire the gun with snap caps. Then I ask how the trigger pulls felt, and this way he can tell me if there is a broken firing pin, or even a broken return spring if the gun has them. I have him make sure the safety works. If the pictures do not show all the external screws on the gun, I ask about them. Buggered slots and improperly timed screws mean an amateur has been poking around inside of the gun. The final questions I ask about are the general wear and tightness of the gun. When the gun is closed, I ask where the top lever is. It's a general rule that the gun could need tightening on the action if the lever is past six o'clock. Next, have the dealer take the fore-end off with the action closed. If the barrels wiggle, the gun is off face and needs to be tightened. Also ask if the forearm is tight. As far as general cosmetics go (pads, grip style, scratches, etc.) it's all a matter of taste, not reliability and good function.

Now you can probably see why I like to use a good gun dealer. The Doug Stewart shakedown is very thorough, and I know exactly what I'm getting. It is very rare that I have any problems with my guns. I own some great guns! People love to buy my guns when I sell them. Buy good guns and they will last you a lifetime and can be great investments. Owning a beautiful side by side that was carefully designed for a special purpose can be as gratifying for a bird hunter as a fine wine can be for a wine connoisseur.

Bird dogs are like the chocolate chips in the cookie of life.

Section XII: Bird Dogs in the Uplands

Owning a bird dog and getting to hunt with one is, dare I say, almost as special and traditional as hunting the uplands with a side by side. This is one of the many joys in my life that my wife introduced me to. This evolution in my life completed my Upland Lifestyle™!

Growing up I had never owned a dog. My mother would not allow any indoor pets. The closest thing I ever had to having my own pet was an outdoor cat that lived in our neighbor's barn. Every boy wishes he could have his own gun and a dog to hunt with. Then, when I grew up, I rented apartments and could not have a dog. My Uncle Mike and I would always just hunt alone. Finally, after hunting with some guides that had dogs, Uncle Mike got a dog one year named Trax. Trax added some neat dynamics to our hunts for many years. Trax put an end to Uncle Mike and I losing crippled birds. Truthfully, I did not know anything about dogs, but I was always intrigued with bird dogs.

This is our famous Llewellyn setter Emma. She is 6 years old now and a hunting machine and more importantly a loving part of our family.

"Part Two"

Back in the mid-1990's I started watching a TV show called "Hunting with Hank." I was totally mesmerized with Dez Young and his Llewellyn Setter, Hank. This dog was amazing at finding and holding birds. I knew this was the missing link in my Upland Lifestyle™. A dog would complete the traditional circle, I'd be able to go hunt public land anywhere and find birds, and I would always have a hunting partner. This Llewellyn Setter was majestic, it had the perfect disposition for me. I loved the "Don't Spoil your Bird Dog" segments. What kind of dog lets you put shades on them and carry them around? The hunting drive was incredible. What a smart, obedient dog! Dez and Hank seemed like they had a connection to the point where Hank seemed to read Dez's mind. You could tell that Dez was in control and Hank was hunting for his master. I wanted this relationship with my own dog, and it had to be a Llewellyn Setter.

God works in mysterious and wonderful ways! Out of nowhere in my life, along comes Jamie. This cute little brunette loved the outdoors and loved animals. One issue, she was a tree hugger from California. I almost didn't date her when I heard she was from California! Thankfully, Jamie is very intelligent and easy to talk to. With some loving common-sense talks, Jamie understood the value of sportsmen and that hunting was important in many logical ways. It didn't take long before she had an appreciation for my passion for hunting and wanted to share my passion with me. Now it gets even weirder, Jamie had two dogs when she met me, one was a German shorthaired pointer and the other was a Labrador retriever. Well, remember that she was a tree hugger from California that didn't hunt. This in turn meant that I inherited two old hunting dogs that didn't hunt, with my new young wife. God must have been in heaven laughing his head off. I finally got bird dogs that don't hunt! But, let's remember that Jamie loves dogs and wants to learn to hunt with her new husband. I started baiting her by watching "Hunting with Hank," and "Dash in the Uplands," I own the entire series on DVD. Jamie started to say things like, "I wish I would have trained my dogs to hunt." And she started to get fascinated with pointing breeds. I think she even started to feel sorry for me not having a dog to hunt with. I was still enamored with setters, but her dogs were really neat dogs.

About four years ago October rolled around and it was time to go hunt woodcock and ruffed grouse in Minnesota at Pineridge Grouse Camp. With a turn of bad fate, Jamie could not take the trip with Uncle Mike and me because her Lab was dying. Being the great woman she is, she insisted that Uncle Mike and I still go hunt in Minnesota. The owners of Pineridge Grouse Camp, Jerry Havel and his father Randy really like my wife and felt bad for her losing a special dog. The entire trip was wearing on my heart for my wife, and I think Jerry noticed it. On my last morning at Pineridge, Jerry and Randy walked over to me at the breakfast table carrying a little Llewellyn setter puppy. Jerry tossed the little dog in my lap and said, "here, bring this dog back to your wife as a gift from me and my dad." I was speechless, my dream dog was in my lap. All kinds of thoughts raced through my head like: I have to drive a thousand miles with this puppy, and I have zero experience training a hunting dog, etc. Jerry proceeded to tell me that we needed a real hunting dog and that this gift would help Jamie get through the loss of her Lab. Jerry has a heart of gold and is a great friend!

It was a long ride home with our new Llewellyn setter. Uncle Mike and I stopped in Southern Minnesota to pheasant hunt. We put the little puppy in a crate in the back of the truck while we hunted. After shooting two pheasants in the field we found out that the puppy loved the dead birds and didn't seem gun shy. We were like two kids with a new puppy. The puppy rode up front in Uncle Mike's lap eating all our snacks with us the whole way home. After traveling almost one thousand miles that puppy could crap through a screen door and not touch a wire. I learned my first lesson about feeding dogs. Did I mention that my wife didn't know I was bringing the dog home? When I pulled up to the house my wife missed me and was standing outside waiting to greet me. I will never forget the joy in her eyes when I pulled the dog out of the car, this made the long drive with a barking, whining, farting, hyper dog worth every mile of it. My wife loves this dog and named her Emma. I think this was the best gift I could ever give her, and at last I have a Llewellyn setter that hunts, thank you God!

Emma is the princess of our house. My wife loads her up in the car and takes her everywhere. Very seldom does a day go by that Jamie won't take Emma for a walk. Jamie even has a pigeon coop with homing pigeons just for Emma. Emma sleeps at the foot of our bed, and she will play and sleep with the cats. Emma has been great for our daughter, Samara, and is very sweet natured. Emma is kind and patient with our cats and totally non-aggressive with other dogs. Emma is just a pure joy with an excellent disposition! I work twelve plus hours a day at a local health club, so Jamie has single handedly trained Emma, and this dog is loyal to her. It is a little embarrassing when we go hunting because Jamie runs the remote and totally controls Emma, and I keep my mouth shut. The TV remote control is all I run. This is our strange arrangement, but it has been great for my wife in the uplands! Our dog (Jamie's dog) is a little quirky, but a sweet dog that finds and points birds in her own way.

Having Emma has added joy to our hunting trips and our lives substantially. Our hunting success has gone up, and the excitement of hunting has gone up. Emma's drive, excitement, and joy of hunting is infectious. I can't wait to see her point every single time. Now when the weather is poor and I'm tired, I'll still hunt just for Emma, and I'm always glad I do. Emma has breathed new life into our hunting trips, I feel like a kid again about hunting. My hunting life has come full circle and is now complete. I shoot classic side by sides, travel the country, hunt with my wife, and have a Llewelyn setter. "Thank you, God," I'm living the dream!

While writing this book Emma got a sister. This is Chloe our new little Llewellyn setter.

Wise men learn from father time!

Section XIII: Different Things I've Learned Over the Years

While writing this book random thoughts raced through my mind that I wanted to share with all my readers. That is why I decided to add this unconventional section at the end of the book. I'm sure many of you have a lot of experience with guns and bird hunting, but this section is worth reading if only one thing resonates with you. Here are a few things I've learned after owning too many guns to count, and forty years of upland bird hunting.

Follow God's path above all others!

Section XIII: Different Things I've Learned Over the Years

A. Being Influenced by Others

About thirty years ago I had saved up enough money to buy another gun. I wanted a sidelock, and nothing else would do. I called a friend of mine, Bill Hanus, to see what he had on hand. Bill had already sold me one of his Ugartechea 28 gauges. Bill knew the build of my body from dealing with me on the Ugartechea. After hearing my price range, Bill told me he had just the perfect gun for me. It was an older AYA model #2 sidelock 20 gauge, it had 26-inch barrels choked skeet, and improved cylinder with double triggers, a straight stalk, and a length of pull of 14 inches. The older AYA's were very well-finished and light weight. I thought the barrels were too short, the chokes sounded too open, too short of pull, and the gun only weighed 5 lbs. 9 oz. Bill told me "nonsense," this would be a perfect sidelock bird gun for me. Bill loved small bores, small shot sizes, and open chokes. This was his motto, using instinctive wing shooting. A lot of people never knew that he was a phenomenal game shot and a side by side guru. I listened to him and bought the gun. The little AYA 20 gauge was absolutely beautiful, I loved this gun. I had been reading all about the Churchill method of shooting, which I had already been using for about ten years. I was single, living alone at the time, so I left the gun out lying on the coffee table and would mount and swing it constantly. Almost every weekend I'd find a way to go shoot. I owned this AYA for a total of four years. The first year I shot the gun very well, the next three years were the most successful of my life! I went an entire hunting season without a single miss with this gun (September - January). Yes, this included dove season and quail season! The gun felt so natural to me that I never thought about it, I'd just throw the gun up and look at the birds. I realize that I was in my prime, fast reflexes, great eyesight, no stress, great focus, and I shot all the time. But I now realize that the gun worked perfectly with my body to bring out my full potential. In defense of the gun, it had perfect trigger pulls, great balance, would produce excellent patterns, and the gun was very fast and comfortable to carry and mount. Bill was right about everything. He told me to err on the short side with the length of pull, learn to be fast and smooth, and shoot lightweight doubles with open chokes and small shot sizes. For the last three years, I could shoot as good as my friend that I mentioned in chapter two. One year before dove season, my client and good friend had me come over to his house to practice shooting. I was very confident, and my shooting was off the chart. My friend started throwing empty shot gun shells through the air, golf balls, lid tops, anything to challenge me. If I could lock my eyes on it, I could hit it. I truly believe that I could have shot with anyone in that period of my life.

By the end of the fourth year of exclusively shooting this small 20 gauge, I had killed more birds than I would ever shoot in my life in a four-year span again. Then I started to feel a strange influence gradually take over my confidence in the little AYA 20 gauge. I started reading all of the great Michael McIntosh books. At about the same time clay target shooting started sweeping the nation. The top experts started to tout heavier guns with long barrels that have more weight to them. This was a way to build in inertia. It started to seem like every time I hunted with someone, they would give me crap about my little toy gun, and say things like "how do you shoot that short little gun?" Then the last straw came on a Nebraska pheasant hunt. A gentleman from the gym that was a self-proclaimed pheasant killer invited me on a hunting trip. Back then I would never pass up a chance to hunt birds, so I gladly went. When we finally got there, I think a little anxiety was setting in on me after hearing his bragging and expertise on hunting for the six-hour drive. Now for the dreaded time to pull out our guns had arrived. Not to my surprise, he pulled out a 12 gauge Remington 870 pump. As he stared at me, I pulled out my little AYA 20 gauge.

He started to laugh and said, "hand me that stagecoach gun." As he mounted and whipped my gun around, he proclaimed that it was a useless toy to hunt wild pheasants with. He said, "with these short barrels and short stock, you better have magnum shells with 4 shot." I said, "don't worry, I know what I'm doing." As he handed my gun back to me, he tossed a 12 gauge 3" magnum shell loaded with 1 5/8 oz. of #4 shot to me. Shaking his head, he stated that he could not believe I brought this gun on a wild pheasant hunt, and that he tossed me a man's shotgun shell. I felt bad and decided I had better not show him my 2 3/4" Federal #6 shot shell that I was going to use. Our first walk was on the edge of a slew. A rooster jumped up in front of me going straight away. I shot and hit the bird, and it started spiraling down out of the air. All of a sudden, I hear a bang to my left and my bird explodes on the way to the ground. He shot my bird as it was falling to the ground. I asked him why he hammered my bird, and he said that it was going to be a cripple. This was a bunch of baloney. He told me the rest of the hunt to stay close to him so he could back me up on my birds. I was very irritated, and decided it was on, and I was going to school this pompous jack wagon. For the next couple of days, I shot every bird that got up so fast that he never even got his gun mounted. I could tell that he was getting irritated. By the second day he told me that I should let the birds get out farther before I shot. I said, "no, maybe you should get a lighter gun and shoot faster." He was speechless. Did I mention that I hit every bird I shot at, with zero cripples? On the long silent ride home, I could feel his resentment towards me. I almost felt bad for Mr. Magnum! Even though my AYA proved worthy, all the backlash seemed to influence me in a negative way towards my beloved 20 gauge.

Now for the total decline of my shooting excellence. I decided to get some shooting lessons and properly gun-fitted by a professional at our local trap range. The instructor fitted me for a gun with a length of pull at 14 1/2 inches and told me to use 28 to 30-inch barrels. Sure, I could hit clay targets, but the gun felt like a cumbersome tree trunk. I kept my mouth shut and tried to learn a few things. After leaving the appointment my mind was confused. I went home and mounted my AYA, it felt different, and the confusion turned to doubt.

I decided to turn to the dark side and trade my AYA 20 gauge in on an Arrieta 16 gauge. Now I had a perfect gun for the uplands according to many experts. The Arrieta 16 gauge was a model 578 with 29-inch barrels, choked tight improved cylinder, and an improved modified. The length of pull was 14 1/2 inches, and the gun weighed 6 lbs. 7oz. Now I had a man's gun with some length and weight. The gun was indeed beautiful in appearance, but it felt barrel heavy and slow to me. Time after time I would get a poor gun mount and shoot over the top of the bird. This gun had the exact dimensions the fitter told me I needed. And believe me I know how to mount a gun. Finally, after two years of poor shooting, I saw the light and sold the gun.

This was a hard lesson that I learned a lot from. Number one was don't fix it if it is not broken. The second thing was not to be influenced by trends or other experts. The third and one of the most important was that I'm an expert and to believe in myself. My techniques in gun handling, gun fit, and gun style work great for me and many others. And there are plenty of experts that side with my general beliefs; Bill Hanus, Robert Churchill, Buz Fawcett, Gough Thomas, and Richard Grozik, to name a few. With all these experts, they will all have a few different opinions. This is okay and very natural. Trust your instincts, as we are using the instinctive method of wing shooting. I love my lightweight doubles that have a low-moment of inertia. Speed is important when upland bird hunting. My short, little doubles are attractive to me in every way, no matter what anyone will say or think. Oddly enough, when a guest looks at my guns, they usually are attracted the most to my E.J. Churchill XXV.

Remember that with trends time will repeat itself, and what goes around comes around.

It is man's natural instinct to hunt!

Section XIII: Different Things I've Learned Over the Years

B. What Hunting Is All About

Hunting is one of our country's richest traditions. Hunting has been bringing family and friends together ever since the beginning of time. The kill is not what hunting is about. Killing a bird has a certain amount of remorse that is felt by all true gentlemen of the uplands. We cherish the birds and put back more than we take. I cherish the birds by making a special meal with them, and by never wasting a bird. I take memorable pictures with them, and I have a few gentlemen that use my feathers to tie flies with. Several of my special birds are mounted in my office so I can have them forever. Most importantly, never shoot more than you need and leave some for the future. I put back to the uplands by donating money for habitat preservation and donate some of my time to help with land projects. I also donate books. As an example, if you are a die-hard pheasant hunter, join Pheasants Forever and donate your time and money to pheasant preservation. Buy your hunting licenses for every state you hunt in and join as many conservation groups as you can.

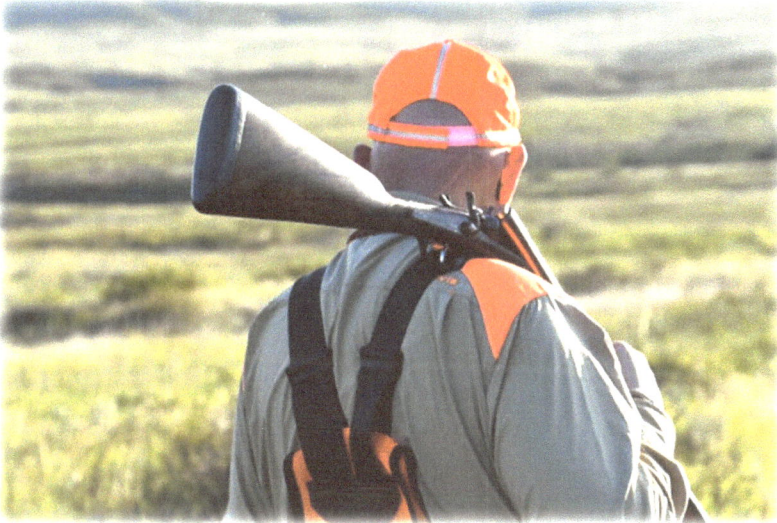

My friend Robert roaming the prairies in South Dakota hunting sharptails, he knows what hunting is all about!

"Part Two"

The charm of hunting is the entire experience as a whole. Get in nature with someone that is special to you and share some beauty that is far away from the city and all the hustle and bustle that goes with everyday life. The only people that get to see all the different upland birds in their natural habitat are hunters. Plus, you get to see all the other special animals that you won't see around urban living. All God's special critters are a gift that we can enjoy.

The best way I can explain how to have a great hunting experience is to give you an example of one of my many hunting trips. Anyone can have a great experience if you will let go and absorb the beauty as Jamie and I did on a dove hunt.

About seven years ago, Jamie and I took a special dove hunt to Maywood, Nebraska. My sister owned a farmhouse there on 190 acres. My sister gave us a key to the farmhouse and told us to go have fun and this was what we were going to do! I remember taking off around noon to head for Nebraska. It was the first week in September and the weather was perfect. We had the best 4 1/2-hour drive ever. We were both excited and had great conversation. About half of the way there we stopped at a convenient store and got some fun junk food, which is very rare for us. Then we listened to some great music and laughed a lot. We enjoy playing name that bird as we drive. I get excited every time I spot a ditch parrot. As you can tell, we love to travel, and sightseeing. We arrived at my sister's property in the early evening. As we drove down her dirt road, we saw two white-tailed deer cross the road in front of us. Then, as we passed by the ten-acre alfalfa field we saw a huge flock of turkeys feeding right in the middle of the field. I clearly remember Jamie asking me where those big turkeys live, I told her in the trees. She could not believe that they could fly, I said trust me. We got settled in and ate some quick sandwiches. A beautiful night walk was in order. I decided that we should take our flashlights and take a nature walk around the property. As we crossed the bridge a mother raccoon and her two big children were hunting in the creek, this was fun to watch as they were turning rocks over, looking for dinner. By the end of the walk we got to see two owls, three deer, and a coyote. I was relaxed, the air was fresh, and all I could hear were crickets and frogs. When I got to the farmhouse, I set our two Parker shotguns on the coffee table, then we snuggled up for a great night's sleep.

The next morning was pure magic. I walked out of the bedroom and instantly saw the two Parkers laying on the coffee table, as I planned. Then I walked out to the kitchen to start some coffee brewing. I looked out the kitchen window and to my surprise there was a covey of Bob White quail feeding underneath the juniper tree in the yard. I called for Jamie, and we both delighted in watching the little birds until they walked off around the house, this was going to be a great day! After a quick breakfast, I grabbed my sister's four-wheeler out of the barn. With our gear and guns strapped down on the front and rear rack we were off to hunt doves. As I drove down the dirt road on the four-wheeler, we saw the same flock of turkeys in the middle of the alfalfa field again. I told my wife to hold on tight and I would show her that turkeys can fly. I sped out into the alfalfa field chasing the flock with the four-wheeler, it was a thrill ride that produced an explosion of flying turkeys. After our fun we headed up to a small pond on the north end of my sister's property. When we pulled up, I hid the four-wheeler in the trees on the south side of the pond. The plan was for me to be on the west side of the pond, and Jamie to be staked out on the east side of the pond. Jamie walked around the pond and flushed a snipe that flew over me and I shot it. Then as she made it to the east side of the pond, she flushed a covey of Bob White quail in the cover that she was going to hide in. Wow, we had seen a snipe and quail but no doves. After about fifteen minutes passed, we started to have a steady stream of doves flying in. The shooting was fast and furious, and we had an absolute ball! We tried to time our shots to keep the doves from falling into the pond, and it worked to an extent. After shooting about twenty plus doves between the two of us, the sky started to get dark with nasty clouds rolling in. I suggested that we take a lunch break in the trees. Halfway through our lunch it started to rain, then an absolute downpour started. We got in the heaviest cover we could find to keep dry, with the Parkers being the biggest concern of course. I kept the guns dry, but we got wet. It was so fun, like two kids out in the rain. The adventure was real, and the storm was a long one. When you are a man with your woman there is always something to do, there is no excuse to be bored! When the rain passed Jamie suggested that we go back to the farm and start a fire to dry out. When we got back Jamie helped me clean the doves. We decided to grill burgers for dinner and sit by the campfire. As we sat by the campfire, we had a few cocktails reminiscing about the days hunt. The stars were amazing, the coyotes were howling, and the frogs and crickets were singing a symphony. This was euphoric and relaxing. For dessert we had some more fun roasting marshmallows over the fire and making smore's. When we went to bed, I was stress free and felt a sense of pure contentment. The next morning, I woke up and sat on the porch drinking my coffee. Jamie scrambled some eggs and cheese with diced dove breast that were seasoned to perfection, what a perfect breakfast. We shot our limits of doves the next day and had a blast. Jamie grilled bacon wrapped dove poppers for dinner with wine, pie and ice-cream for dessert. We cuddled up for a movie and popcorn after dinner. I did not want to leave. Jamie and I felt closer than ever. This was like a honeymoon, even better without all the people and hassle of airports that most honeymoon trips deal with. It was the whole experience, not just killing. It was about getting out in nature away from buildings, traffic, computers, cellphones, and other people. It is special to go where animals outnumber the people. This is hunting in the uplands in its's purest form. I choose to do this with special people, special guns, special dogs, in special places, all to make special memories! This is what hunting is all about!

Section XIII: Different Things I've Learned Over the Years

C. Extra Bits & Pieces

1. Square Loads

I am going to discuss some odds and ends about cartridges. First, lately I have read how some experts are claiming that a balanced square load is irrelevant nowadays that there is hard shot and plastic shot cups. This is over-stated! Yes, shot cups made of plastic have reduced shot strings, as hard shot has also helped. Michael McIntosh was correct about shot strings and the beauty of a square load. This is why a 1-ounce load is so effective in a 16 gauge, or why a 3/4-ounce load is like magic in a 28 gauge. A few months ago, Morris Baker and I had a great talk about the effectiveness of our 2-inch 12 gauges because of the short shot strings. My now passed dear friend W. J. knew all about shot strings. W. J. designed gun powder for Federal and was a professional skeet shooter for Federal. I learned a lot from W. J. and miss him dearly. He was always stressing how important a short shot string was on fast crossing shots at quail, grouse, and woodcock. Through McIntosh and W.J. teachings, I learned some important things that have proven to be true. First, is that a large bore of a 12 gauge is much more forgiving than smaller bores. Usually the so-called experts will do all their tests with 12 gauges. A 12 gauge will produce a fairly short shot string with 1 1/2-ounce shot, and sometimes with even a little more shot. But the 3 1/2-inch 12 gauge loaded with 2-ounce shot is a nightmare. Even in a 12 gauge when the column height is too great, shot gets damaged. And, these loads produce too much pressure that damages the shot at the bottom of the load due to excessive setback pressure. Another factor regarding long shot strings is the length of the shot charge going down the barrel. The length gets exaggerated very quickly, and the pellets will have a high degree of varied speeds among the longer string. In a square load you will have a great core of pellets flying at the same speed. Ask any professional sporting clay shooter if they think they would break more clays with a 12-gauge load that contained 1 1/2-ounce shot. I'm sure the answer would be no, that a 1 1/8-ounce load is more effective at clay target ranges because of the shot string being short and effective. More is not better! 1-ounce loads are becoming more and more popular. Smaller bores damage more shot, this puts an importance on smaller shot charges. I have a lot of experience shooting 28 gauges and so did McIntosh and my friend W. J. We all agree that the 3/4-ounce loads are of magic in the 28 gauge. 1-ounce loads ruin the soft recoiling bolts of lightning that the 3/4-ounce loads produce. No matter how hard the lead shot is, or how great the plastic shot cup is, a 1-ounce 28-gauge load will damage the shot and produce a longer shot string, with a lot of extra recoil. Many will argue that they want a number 5 shot load in their 28 gauge for pheasant hunting, and a 1-ounce load contains more shot, and that a large pheasant doesn't need to be shot with a short shot string. Only part of this argument is true. A short shot string is most advantageous on small targets that are crossing at a high speed. The rest of the argument falls apart with common knowledge of ballistics. A 28 gauge does not pattern #5 shot well at all. So, adding an extra 1/4-ounce of shot that is all going to get damaged anyway, will only add to crippling more birds. Most 28 gauges will not pattern loads well with a shot size larger than 7 1/2 shot. I've had a few that will pattern good with 6 shot, but it's rare, and none of mine have produced good patterns with 5 shot! Small bores need small shot sizes. If you want to hunt pheasants with #5 shot, use a 12 gauge or a 16 gauge, period. Do not try to make small bores work for large game birds at long ranges. Small bores are meant for small game birds at close range. Remember these two important facts: large shot resists deforming much better than small shot, and large shot patterns better in large bores.

After this discussion on short shot strings and the effectiveness of having one, I want to discuss optimum loads. Like anything in life, ammo has a perfect balance. More is not better, and sometimes too little is not better. I'm going to use my 2-inch 12 gauge as an example. I like to shoot RST loads that contain 15/16-ounce shot. This load produces beautiful patterns, and the recoil is very minimal. The shot string is so short that no upland game bird could fly fast enough to not get hit by the entire pattern. Now RST does offer a 2-inch 12 gauge load with 7/8-ounce shot, or a load with 3/4-ounce shot. I personally feel that a 3/4-ounce load is not going to have a shorter shot string that could ever be noticed or beneficial unless you're taking crossing shots at hummingbirds. A 15/16-ounce load in a 2-inch 12 gauge is perfect, and a 3/4-ounce load is losing pattern density. If recoil is the reason for choosing a 3/4-ounce load, then remember that there is always the sport of golf for these people. Find a happy medium between a nice short shot string and great pattern density. Let me give you a Doug Stewart analogy. If you have a migraine headache, a wise man might take about three aspirin. The more is better guy might take six to eight aspirin and get sick with a bleeding ulcer. Then, the less is more guy might take half an aspirin and get zero results. This is a great example of optimum dose, enough said. Since there are more 12 gauge shooters out there than any other gauge, I'll tell you about a very balanced load that will pattern great in almost any 12 gauge with almost any choke. A 12 gauge 2 3/4-inch 3 1/4-dram equiv. with 1 1/4-ounce shot that produces a muzzle velocity of approximately 1,220 FPS. This load has fairly short shot strings with great pattern density with everything from #9 shot to #4 shot. As always, I suggest using extra hard shot. If you up the velocity, it might be advantageous to use extra hard shot that is plated with 10 microns of nickel, or pellets plated with 15 microns of copper. Live pigeon shooters have sworn by this load for decades. One last secret is to use the best trap loads and pigeon loads in the uplands. These competitive loads use the best components and produce the best patterns. Competitive clay shooters have a lot of money riding on their scores and have always demanded the best ammo. God's special animals deserve nothing less than clean humane kills. To help you choose optimum loads for each gauge, I designed a chart that has the minimum and maximum charge of shot that should be used in each gauge along with the minimum and maximum size of shot that should be fired through each bore size.

Gauge	Optimum Shot Charges	Optimum Size of Shot (Lead)
12	7/8 oz min - 1 1/4 oz max	#10 shot min - #4 shot max
16	7/8 oz min - 1 1/16 oz max	#10 shot min - #5 shot max
20	3/4 oz min - 1 oz max	#9 shot min - #5 shot max
28	3/4 oz min - 7/8 oz max	#8 1/2 shot min - #6 shot max

Gauge	Common Proven English Optimum Loads	Shot Sizes
12	1 1/16 oz	6, 7, 7 1/2
16	1 oz	7, 7 1/2, 8
20	7/8 oz	7 1/2, 8
28	3/4 oz	7 1/2, 8

NOTE: The charts represent loads for upland birds. The English optimum chart represents the ultimate choice for short shot strings and even patterns in each gauge.

Section XIII: Different Things I've Learned Over the Years

C. Extra Bits & Pieces

2. Field Tips

Now that we all are properly shooting our traditional side by sides with gentlemen cartridges, the harvest of special upland birds is the gift. I feel it is fitting to make a few notes about birds.

Two quick field dressing techniques come to mind. The first is to take out a pocketknife with a blade and a gut hook. Mine is a Boker, but there are several other knife makers that make bird knives with a hook and a blade. Pluck a few feathers out around the bird's vent so you can make a clean cut above the vent. Open up the body cavity with a lateral cut. Now take the gut hook and pull the entrails out. Make sure all the innards are out, then stuff a handful of grass into the body cavity and you're done. Keep the birds fairly cool and out of the sun. The birds will keep until you get home. Remember that the British hang their pheasants for up to two weeks for aging. Just draw the entails and let the body cavity cool.

The second technique I use for field dressing a bird is even faster, as long as the bird is still warm. The bird must be of the larger species with strong wings like pheasants, grouse, and chuckars. I lie the bird on the ground belly up with both wings out to the sides, I firmly plant my right foot on the right wing and my left foot on the left wing. Then I grab the bird's feet and pull slowly and firmly upwards never stopping until the bird's head is pulled through its body cavity. If done properly, you should be standing there holding the entire bird, except the breast and two wings lying on the ground. The innards will be pulled out and all you have to do is clip the wings off the breast. You can use the legs if you choose.

The Traditional Side by Side

"Part Two"

Dealing with crippled birds in the most humane, quick, and painless way is an absolute must. About twenty-five years ago, I learned a way to dispatch cripples from Michael McIntosh. Grasp the bird by the back with your thumb and forefinger on either side of the spine between its ribs and the wings. Pinch in hard under the spine, sometimes you can even feel your fingers touch, hold the pressure; in a few seconds the bird will flutter and then quietly pass. The pressure paralyzes the heart and lungs. Ringing a bird's neck never went well for me, sometimes it didn't work at all, or I'd get carried away and rip the head off. My way is humane, works every time, and leaves an unruffled bird. We should all try to be as respectful as possible with these special birds.

Section XIII: Different Things I've Learned Over the Years

C. Extra Bits & Pieces

3. Gear

After 40 years of upland bird hunting in almost every state and in almost every weather condition, I have learned a lot about the attire I like to wear. Being properly dressed can be the difference between a great hunt and a complete disaster.

Starting from the ground up, it's important to have a great pair of boots. In the fall, logging trails and the woods in Minnesota are muddy with water everywhere. I wear a pair of time proven L.L. Bean rubber boots. They're uglier than sin, but the boots are rugged and totally waterproof. I also wear them when hunting in snowy conditions. When I'm hunting in the wide-open prairies, desert, or just general upland hunting in moderate to warm weather, I like to wear a pair of Kangarro upland bird boots. I have found these boots to be the lightest weight, rugged, and excellent for comfort, preventing blisters, and fatigue. Always make sure your boots fit properly and are waterproof.

"Part Two"

When bird hunting, the socks you wear are just as important as the boots you wear. In warm weather you need a sock that will wick moisture away from your feet and keep them cool. As always, you'll need a sock that prevents blisters and will cushion your feet with excellent arch support. The socks cannot slip and bunch up, and they must be tough enough to stand up to miles and miles of intense hiking. I use socks that are made for hikers in warm weather. These socks will usually be made using a mixture of spandex, polyester, and cotton. When hunting in the cold I switch out my socks to a thicker pair of wool blend socks. The best blend will use merino wool, nylon, and lycra. My feet never get cold using the right socks and the right boots. A little secret that I swear by is I roll on a little antiperspirant deodorant onto my feet (especially around my heels, toes and balls of feet) before I put on my socks each morning. This puts a stop to blisters and helps keep your feet comfortable in all weather conditions.

Moving up to the pants. I've tried about every kind of pants out there and now I use only one style. I wear tough field pants that have a rugged, cotton canvas sown into the pant legs which reinforces the legs. These pants resist briars and thorns with ease and are treated with a water repellant. I also treat my pants with a tick repellant once a year. When the weather turns cold, I simply wear a pair of long johns underneath my field pants.

On my upper body I layer my shirts. I do not wear bulky jackets. In warm weather I wear a thin long sleeve shirt made with a polyester/cotton blend. The polyester is what you always want against your skin. Polyester wicks moisture away from your skin, dries instantly, and will allow air flow. Do not make 100% cotton your first layer. On cold days I make my first layer a long sleeve shirt made with a polyester/nylon blend. The polyester wicks moisture away from the skin, and the tight weave of nylon holds your body's heat in. Then I add additional layers of shirts. Wool, cotton, and fleece are all good choices. On really cold days I make my last shirt a long sleeve made of cotton/nylon/spandex blend. This shirt is tightly woven and very dense. The tight weave of nylon and spandex will stop the wind, keep the heat in, and is also waterproof. Layering your shirts is very effective. When I layer my shirts correctly, I have great mobility compared to wearing a bulky jacket. This is vital to fast and correct gun mounting. When you properly layer your shirts, air and heat get trapped between the layers and keep you warmer, and the wind has a harder time penetrating the layers. When I get hot, I simply shed a layer. If I get cold, I simply add a layer.

When I was young, I hated to wear hats. Now that I'm older, I have learned to wear them. On warm sunny days I wear my old traditional full brimmed western style hat. This hat keeps my head cool and the full brim protects my eyes, face, and head from the sun. In addition, the hat is waxed and waterproof. When woodcock and grouse hunting in the thick woods, I wear a blaze orange ball cap to be visible.

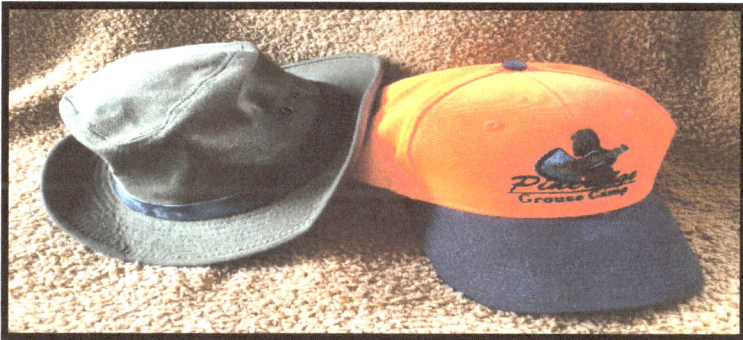

The Traditional Side by Side

"Part Two"

When the weather turns cold enough, I reluctantly wear a stocking cap that has an extra fold over my ears to keep them warm. I don't like having my hearing muffled, but I've learned how much heat escapes through your head.

A bird hunter could wear gloves in all seasons. I'm learning to wear them more and more. A thin, soft leather shooting glove has many benefits. Shooting gloves protect your hands from the hot sun and from a hot set of barrels. Gloves also protect your gun from the harmful effects of the salt and oils in our skin. In addition, the gloves help with gripping the gun and protect your hands against briars and thorns. As you have probably already guessed, I waterproof all my gloves. For the really cold days, I wear some leather shooting gloves that are fleece lined. The gloves have the dexterity to work my double triggers and safety, but only work to about 20 degrees Fahrenheit. When the temperature drops low, I break open a little hand warmer and stuff one in each cuff, then I'm good to go.

For many years I tried to wear different kinds of shooting vests, all with the same results. The vests all pulled on my neck, got caught on branches, the straps and hanging weight interrupted a proper gun mount, and they were bulky and hot. For the last twenty-five years I've worn a game bird belt. I love it and I will never go back to a vest. My belt has two side pouches and one large pouch in the rear. The game pouch in the rear will hold three pheasants, max. I have a knife and mini flashlight attached on the belt. I put my shells for my right barrel in the right pouch and shells for my left barrel in the left pouch. The pouches have a flap and are all waterproof. Usually I carry a couple of water bottles and snacks in the back pouch. This rugged canvas, waxed belt is very comfortable. The belt is light weight and does not affect my gun mount, or any other movements. In the winter the belt protects my ammo with quick access and the belt works great with any clothing.

My wife, Jamie, is the dog handler so like many of you, she wears a vest. My Uncle Mike customized her vest to fit her in the most comfortable way possible. Jamie loads her vest with everything but the kitchen sink. I'll try to list at least 90% of the things she has found to be necessary. On her left shoulder strap Mike sowed a neat clear plastic pouch on it to perfectly hold her remote. Then on the right strap, just below her chest to not interfere with her gun mount, Mike sowed on another clear pouch to hold her cell phone. These have proven to provide quick access and to be convenient. The rest of the vest contains: first aid kit, Leatherman knife, leash, compass, small flashlight, energizing dog treats, water for the dog, a whistle, a bell, snacks, her water bladder, shotgun shells, lip balm, etc. I'm sure glad that she is the dog handler!

In this section, I simply wanted to share with you what works for me. I purposely did not give a lot of brands on the clothing. Brands do not matter, as we all have different budgets and opinions on brands. It is not necessary to look like you just walked out of an Orvis magazine. Often, I look like I walked out of the 1920's. Comfort and function are all that matters, this is why I gave specific fabric blends and how to use them. This is the beauty of the uplands; you can just be yourself. When you're away from the city and all the people, there is no one to impress or please. The birds could care less how you look! In the uplands you are free, so find what truly matters to you and what little things might add special touches to your trip. I personally love the old traditional way of upland bird hunting, even in some of my clothing.

*A body in motion stays in motion ...
your waistline is your lifeline!*

Section XIII: Different Things I've Learned Over the Years

D. Being in Shape

Upland bird hunting is a special way of life that can be enjoyed for your entire lifetime. When I was young, it was exciting to shoot guns and get as many birds as possible. Now that I'm older, I enjoy fine guns, beautiful scenery, special birds, and the adventure with my loved ones. I cherish having a glass of wine or whisky after the hunt, taking the time to reminisce around the campfire about the days hunt. Hunting means more to me than ever. For this reason, I will stay in shape as long as possible so I can keep hunting and making more memories as someday those memories will be all I will have left.

Hunting the uplands is hard work. You can walk from sunrise to sunset in unforgiving terrain and in any weather condition. To add to the long hunt, you will be carrying a gun and weighted down with ammo, water, food, etc. I usually hunt for about three days in a row and cover 30-40 miles depending on the cover. Being in shape is a must! When you are in shape, the hunt is much more enjoyable, and you are also less likely to get injured. If you plan on hunting as you get older, a normal exercise program should be followed regularly.

I'm not writing a book on health or trying to preach to anyone, I just think we can all enjoy our guns and hunting more and for longer if we can all stay in shape. Jamie and I are both health and fitness trainers for a living. I'm sure my job makes me more aware of the benefits of exercise in sports and in activities than most people.

When hunting hard the feet, knees, hips, and lower back take a lot of abuse. The first step is to lose any extra body fat. By simply losing 10-15 lbs. you can reduce thousands of accumulated pounds of pressure on your joints. Your leg muscles will also thank you. Cardio conditioning will help prevent fatigue, and strong leg muscles are a must to climb and propel you through cover. To accomplish all this, a good sound diet needs to be followed, with exercise.

Eating a healthy diet that is well-balanced with whole grains, fruit, nuts, vegetables, and lean protein will give you energy and keep you strong for life. Cardio exercise such as walking fast, biking, hiking, ellipticals, rowing, swimming, stair climbers, etc., are all good sources of cardio. Cardiovascular exercise is great for heart health. When cardio exercise is done on a regular basis, an increase in the body's overall energy levels and endurance levels will be noticed. Body fat will become more controllable. General weight training is good for muscle strength, and to help preserve bone mass. It is biblical to have our lives in balance. Balance in everything we do is the key. I cannot explain it any better than that!

Feel free to contact me or Jamie if you need help with diet or exercise. My wife not only trains people at our local gym, she is a certified instructor at the Good Samaritan for elders. Jamie and I help coach people on-line all over the United States. Be fit and ready for uplands!

To shoot side by sides in the uplands is like being the gatekeeper of time.

Section XIII: Different Things I've Learned Over the Years

E. My Attraction to the Traditional Side by Side

In the general sense of the word, side by sides are undeniably attractive. A well-proportioned side by side is sleek with nice lines and a lively feel. Other designs of shotguns have large forearms, magazines, tall ribs, big pistol grips, bulky stocks, etc. Being the last chapter in this book it feels fitting to give one more Doug Stewart analogy. I suppose beauty is always in the eye of the beholder. I remember back in high school having a friend that received a Gremlin for his first car. This was the ugliest car I had ever seen! My friend thought this was the coolest car ever. I'm sure there are plenty of bird hunters that can see the beauty in a shotgun that would serve better as a boat oar.

The Traditional Side by Side

"Part Two"

My attraction to the traditional side by side goes beyond visual beauty and feel. Beauty is only skin deep, but ugly goes clear to the bone. Upland bird hunting is special, and side by sides are special. Side by sides go with upland bird hunting like salt goes with pepper. Look on any dining room table in almost any country and more often than not you will see a salt and pepper shaker. These two spices complement each other. Salt and pepper are the gold standard in spices. Now look at old paintings of upland bird hunting from any country. Look through old books on bird hunting. I remember looking at guns in pawn shops when I was young, and my grandfather's gun cabinet. Old shows would use side by sides when bird hunting. Side by sides were always associated with upland bird hunting and could be seen in all these places. Side by sides are the gold standard in upland bird guns! Side by sides are no longer the most prevalent, or even the most respected, but they are the gold standard among sportsman that know the difference and care. Side by sides exude class, craftsmanship, and tradition. The simplicity, reliability, beauty, and feel of side by sides will always be the best design of shotguns for upland bird hunting. Some things in life cannot be improved upon and should not be.

Side by side enthusiasts seem to be a different breed of bird hunters. Instead of being killers, they are a passionate bunch of gentlemen that appreciate the finer things in life. Why not be passionate about everything in the uplands. The more we can absorb great guns, great dogs, great places, and great birds, with great people the more fulfillment can be experienced from the uplands. Why not support traditional side by sides and what they stand for and represent? I personally want to preserve upland bird hunting the way it has always been, especially in this ever-changing world. Think about how guns have changed. Picture a new modern factory that produces auto loaders, pumps, and over/under shotguns. The guns are all machine made with modern machines that duplicate every gun exactly the same way.

Most of the machinists do not even hunt and are basically assembly line workers. The factory workers are not gun builders, they simply run their machine. The art of gun building is dying. Now the guns are really built by computers and duplicated in high numbers for general use, not upland bird hunting. Guns of today are only as precise as machining tolerances allow for. Now we have synthetic stocks, laser and stamped engraving, screw in chokes, and parts that are crudely fitted all with synthetic finishes. Even the checkering is done by a machine. I immediately notice the poor wood to metal fit, all the waves and ripples in the finishes, poor trigger pulls, bad balance and feel, and just an overall cheap, fake, artificial look. In contrast, skilled gunsmiths knew how to use reamers, emery cloth, files, chisels, blades, and their hands to polish and rub in oil. Think about all the regulating, bone charcoal case hardening, and hand engraving. How much hand fitting do you think goes into the modern guns? I routinely hunt with a few side by sides that are over 130 years old. Do you think today's modern factory-made guns will still be in use 130 years from now? We should still demand quality today! I could go on and on, but I think my point is obvious. My guns are works of art that I enjoy looking at in the field and at home. Out of respect, a beautiful bird deserves to be shot with a beautiful gun.

Old craftsmen that made quality side by sides tried to make the best bird guns possible. Building a gun should be done by a man with a passion and skill, the gun will emulate this. A modern gun built by a programmed machine will also imitate how it was made. What kind of gun are you going to pass on as an heirloom when you die? I'm just a caretaker of my guns until the next gentleman gets them. I hope to pass on a passion in the uplands with my traditional side by sides and all they stand for and represent! The traditional side by side always was and always will be, king of the upland bird guns!

In Closing

"Some of my simple rules that I live by being a side by side enthusiast and lifelong upland bird hunter."

1.) I always try to hunt with a side by side that has a special meaning to me.

2.) I use light loads like the British. The British know that the best way to kill a bird is to put the shot in the proper place, not how much shot or how fast it gets there.

3.) Use the most open choke that can get the job done.

4.) Use the smallest size shot that can get the job done.

5.) I limit my shooting to shots under 40 yards.

6.) Great shooting for me is all about being able to keep my eyes focused on the leading edge of the target, and having my hands and body do what my eyes and brain are telling them to without conscious thought. I must shoot subconsciously!

7.) Hunting is a rich tradition that has been going on since the beginning of man, so I always try to give back more to the uplands than I take.

8.) I always have a great time and cherish every hunt that I take, as I never know when I have taken my last shot.

9.) I try to be a gentleman and treat others as I'd like to be treated.

10.) I thank God every day for the things that I am grateful for. Life is all about choices. I choose to be happy.

11.) We are all God's children. It is important to play and have hobbies that we are passionate about. This gives us something to look forward to and helps get us through tough times.

12.) Tough times don't last, tough people do!

13.) Don't worry about anything, pray about everything!

14.) I try to keep everything in my life in good balance. I've mentioned it before, that balance is the key to life. I see too much radicalism nowadays. We should all have a sensible balance in work, play politics, religion, health, etc. Knowledge without wisdom is worthless. I'm working on my out of balance love for side by sides. I suppose we all have some things out of balance! Maybe my next book will be about over/unders…..don't hold your breath.

Index

"Dealers of English guns that can make sure you're getting a safe gun that is in-proof."

1.) Vintagedoubles.com (Kirby Hoyt); Phone No. (509) 665-7675

Comments: I've used Kirby a lot in my later years. Kirby is an honest man and has some of the best prices out there. Kirby has one of the biggest selections, he will work with you.

2.) Hillrodandgun.com; Phone No. (406) 585-2228

Comments: They specialize in lightweight English doubles like I like. Their prices are amazing.

3.) Champlinfirearms.com (George Caswell); Phone No. (580) 237-7388

Comments: George is an expert in English guns and has a passion for them. George always has some good guns on hand and has his guns fairly priced.

4.) Woodcockhill.com (Glenn Baker); Phone No. (570) 864-3242

Comments: I have a soft spot for old Glenn. Glenn sold me my first English gun and turned me on to R.S.T. shells before they were a company. Glenn always has some great guns and he is an expert in English guns. Glenn and I both love 2-inch 12 bores!

5.) Griffinhowe.com; Phone No. (973) 398-2670

Comments: This company is expensive, but first rate all the way. Griffin and Howe have true English class, they even import the best new English guns like Boss.

Index

"Wing shooting instruction and gun fitting."

1.) Varneysclaysports.com (Brad Varney - "The down east Yankee"); Richmond, Maine; Phone No. (207) 737-4993

Comments: Brad is my kind of guy. He has been shooting longer than I have. Brad is simple, he believes as I do in using your senses, foremost your eyes. His instruction is affordable and easy to learn. Brad also has a book out called "Maine-Ly Wing Shooting."

2.) Fieldsportltd.com; Phone No. (231) 933-0767

Comments: Bryan Bilinski is a great guy and has an excellent wing shooting class.

3.) Skyhorsepublishing.com (Buz Fawcett); "Buz Fawcett's Wing Shooting Workshop"

Comments: Buz is an old school instructor out of Idaho. His school teaches the instinctive method and is one of the best! I'm not sure if he still teaches or not. If he doesn't you can still get his book. Buz and I see eye to eye on gun fit and shooting!

4.) Woodcockhill.com; Phone No. (570) 864-3242

Comments: They have a great affordable class. They teach a style of the Churchill method. You will leave a better shot all the way around. Gun fitting is part of the class.

5.) Griffinhowe.com; Phone No. (973) 398-2670

Comments: Well known, first class. True modern English instruction.

Index: Join These

"Special Organizations that Support Upland Birds"

We must support and donate for the future of bird hunting. If you hunt the bird, it makes sense to give back and support that bird!

1.) Pheasantsforever.org

2.) Quailforever.org/duffle

3.) Ruffedgrousesociety.org; Phone No. (412) 262-4044

4.) Woodcocklimited.org; Phone No. (570) 435-3487

5.) www.sharptails.org (Minnesota)

6.) Projectupland.com

7.) Trcp.org Theodore Roosevelt Conservation Partnership

8.) NRA

9.) Grousepartners.org

10.) Backcountryhunters.org (BHA)

They help preserve hunting and fishing on public lands.

Index

"Special organizations for side by side enthusiasts.

Very important for the future of side by sides."

1.) Parkerguns.org (PGCA); Phone No. (207) 646-2219

2.) Lcsmith.org; L.C. Smith Collectors Association

3.) Lefevercollectors.com

4.) Foxcollectors.com

5.) The German Gun Collectors Association

www.ingramcontent.com/pod-product-compliance
Lightning Source LLC
Chambersburg PA
CBHW041959090426
42811CB00030B/1960/J

9 780578 753874